LOVE
One
ANOTHER

Gordon Ferguson

LOVE
One
ANOTHER

Illumination Publishers

Love One Another: The Importance and Power of
Christian Relationships (New Edition)

© 2013 by Gordon Ferguson and Illumination Publishers

Printed in the United States of America.

ISBN: 978-1-939086-20-4

Unless otherwise indicated, all Scripture references are from the Holy
Bible, New International Version, copyright 1973, 1978, 1984 by the
International Bible Society. Used by permission of Zondervan Bible
Publishers.

Cover and interior book design: Toney Mulhollan.

About the author: Gordon Ferguson is a graduate of Northwestern State University and the
Harding Graduate School of Religion, with a
master's degree in New Testament studies. Having more than 40 years of experience, he has
served as an evangelist, elder and teacher. Since
beginning his teaching ministry full time, he has
focused on training ministers in the U.S., Eurasia and Asia, emphasiz-
ing leadership training and biblical exposition. Gordon has also written twelve books and has many audio/video teaching series available.
He and his wife, Theresa, now live in Los Angeles, California, where
Gordon directs the Pacific School of Ministry. For more articles and
information see Gordon's web site at www.GFTM.org.

Illumination Publishers International
www.ipibooks.com
6010 Pinecreek Ridge Court
Spring, Texas 77379-2513

Contents

DEDICATION

The material in *Love One Another* was first printed many years ago, but has continued to resonate with church leaders because of the practical relevancy of the material. Theresa and I became a part of what we then called the Discipling Movement back in 1985, and what we have taught about loving one another as Jesus commanded has been simply our desire to pass on what we have ourselves received in this movement of churches. Bottom line, we have been loved unconditionally by so many leaders and members alike that it would be impossible to list all of those who have been used by God to change our hearts and lives in ways known fully only by Him. Therefore, this new edition of *Love One Another* is dedicated to those multitudes of individual disciples who have taught us to love more like the Master and who will forever reside deeply within our hearts.

INTRODUCTION

Christianity is a religion of *relationships*. Jesus said that both he and the work that he came to do would be judged by the manner in which his disciples related to one another (John 13:34–35). The whole Bible is all about relationships. In summarizing the contents of the Old Testament, Jesus said that it distilled down to loving God with our entire being and loving our neighbor as we love ourselves (Matthew 22:36-40). God's revelation, Old Testament or New Testament, is designed to teach us how to love in the way that he loves, and to motivate us to relate with one another on earth in the manner in which he relates to the inhabitants of heaven itself!

The Bible focuses on relationships at four levels: relationship between man and his Maker; relationship within the physical family; relationship between God's children, and the relationship of his children to the ones who are not yet his children. All of these areas are highly important, and very large portions of Scripture are aimed at each of them. Our task in this booklet (and in the tapes which accompany it) is to narrow the study down to the level of how God's children are to relate to one another. With this narrower focus, my desire is to provide a fairly in-depth study, in extended outline form, of just what God wants Christian relationships to be like.

Two chapters are specifically dealing with *one another* relationships, but actually all of the chapters are covering some aspect of these types of relationships. Most religious groups are declining and dying because they have no real *one another* relationships within their particular group. God works in our lives *primarily* through the people in our lives. And if we do not have significant spiritual relationships with each other in the church, we cease to *be* the church. A church without spiritual relationships (as defined by the Bible) cannot *attain* spirituality as a group in the first place, and whatever degree of spirituality might be discovered by some individuals cannot be long *maintained* without one another religion as its basis.

Life has little to do with possessions, accomplishments, entertainment, and related pursuits, in spite of the fact that those things are what our present society seems to be hungering and thirsting after! Life has *everything* to do with relationships. As Moses said long ago, "Choose life so that you and your children may live (Deuteronomy 30:19)." Life lived according to God's plan is the *abundant* life that Jesus came to give. Life lived according to any other plan is mere existence at best and misery at worst. Therefore, choose the way of life designed by God, which is to say, choose life that is so deeply entwined within the Christian fellowship that all who see us will say *"See how they love one another!"*

CHAPTER ONE

LOVE:
Damaged by Worldly Relationships

INTRODUCTION

1. The difficulty of loving like Jesus is a huge challenge, not only because he is our perfect model to imitate (1 John 2:6), but because we have learned about love in all the wrong places.

2. Before we can love in the correct way, we must see where our concepts are incorrect because of our training in the world.

3. In this first lesson, we will examine what worldly concepts of love are, and just how our past worldliness has damaged our present ability to love as God loves.

4. In this way, we can get rid of the past baggage and replace it with the type of love that God has called us to *feel* and to *practice* on a consistent basis.

5. For our purposes, two passages on worldliness (sin) will help us to understand just how our experiences in the world have limited our abilities to have deep and godly relationships. These passages are Romans 1:18–32 and 2 Timothy 3:1–5 (the first one centers more on the sins of the irreligious and the second includes more of the sins normally associated with religious types).

6. Note that in the Romans passage, the path into deeper and deeper sins began with humanism (trust in the wisdom of man) and the loss of gratitude for the blessings that God provides.

7. Read both texts before we proceed with the categories of sins which have most impacted our relationships.

I. Worldliness Through Misused Sexuality

A. Biblical teaching

1. In Romans 1, once men had become humanistic and ungrateful, the text says that God *"gave them over."* In fact, this phrase is used three times (vv 24, 26, 28).

   a. The first use of the phrase shows that they became sexually impure and immoral. Once God is taken out of the picture, the strength of the sexual drive naturally leads into its misuse and abuse.

   b. The second time God gave them over, they progressed into sexual perversion—homosexuality.

   c. The third time God gave them over, they became enmeshed in all kinds of sins.

2. Other important New Testament passages about immorality and homosexuality are 1 Corinthians 6:9–10 and 2 Peter 2:14–15.

   a. In the 1 Corinthians passage, sexual sins are very specifically denoted.

      (1) "Sexually immoral" is from *porneia*, a broad term for sexual activity outside the marriage relationship, whether before or after marriage.

      (2) "Adultery" is from *moicheia*, which refers to sexual activity in an illicit relationship with at least one of the parties being married.

      (3) "Male prostitutes" is from *malakos*, translated *effeminate* in the KJV, likely referring to the more passive partner in a homosexual relationship.

(4) Homosexual offenders would be the more dominant partners in a sexual act with another of their same sex.

b. In the 2 Peter passage, the consuming nature of immorality is described with the phrase *"eyes full of adultery."* This provides a very accurate description of a large segment of our society today. Bottom line, they have sex on the brain and it colors much of their thought processes much of the time.

B. Practical impact on relationships

1. When much of our relating to the opposite sex has had sexual overtones, a number of hindrances may develop.

   a. Lustful thoughts toward one another even in the church can be a problem.

   b. Hugs and other demonstrations of affection can cause feelings of uneasiness until we grow in this area.

   c. We may project a flirtatious spirit without being fully aware of it. Warmth is a wonderful thing, but it must be holy warmth!

   d. Mistrust of others' motives can arise because we read *our former* motives into their attitudes or actions (and we may well be off-base by a large amount).

   e. In short, we just have to learn how to relate to the opposite sex in the way that Jesus did it—as close spiritual friends. And we must avoid judging others' motives on the basis of what our own motives were in the world.

2. The approach to changing these worldly hindrances is not complicated.

   a. Be open with God and with others about what is really going on inside your heart and mind. Be blatantly honest with both God and others—Satan cannot thrive in the light.

b. Avoid circumstances that would play into your present weaknesses.

c. Keep asking for much advice about relating to the opposite sex and then follow it.

d. Pray for a change of mind and heart, and it will come.

II. Worldliness Through Materialism

A. Biblical teaching

1. In the Romans 1 passage, two of the sins listed relate directly to the overall problem of materialism—*greed* and *envy* (v 29).

2. In 2 Timothy 3:2, the people are described as *"lovers of money."*

3. One of the best places in the Bible to learn about materialism is from the Gospel of Luke. This book was written to a gentile audience with a major emphasis on the subject of repentance. As might be expected, it often deals specifically with the subject of money.

   a. In chapter 2, the birth of Jesus in a stable and the offering of doves for his consecration showed the poverty of the family into which he was born. Surely this was designed to teach a major lesson about values in life!

   b. In 3:7-14, John the Baptist defines repentance in very specific terms.

      (1) Sharing possessions

      (2) Honesty in obtaining money

      (3) Being content with one's salary

   c. In 6:20–38, our attitudes toward money are exposed.

(1) A rich/poor contrast is made in vv 20–21 and 24–25.

(2) Give and lend to others, even if you think they will not repay you (vv 27–36). If we live in fear that we will be taken advantage of, then we do not live with trust in God, and we do not live *like* God.

(3) Finally, give generously and you will receive generously (v 38).

d. In 8:14, through the words of the Parable of the Sower, we are told that our spiritual lives can be choked out by life's worries, *riches* and pleasures.

e. In 12:13–21, we find the Parable of the Rich Fool.

(1) The parable begins with a man wanting to make sure that he received the portion of the inheritance due him.

(2) The immediate answer of Jesus was: "Watch out! Be on your guard against all kinds of greed; a man's life does not consist in the abundance of his possessions."

(3) Then he ends the parable with these words in v 21: "This is how it will be with anyone who stores up things for himself but is not rich toward God."

f. In 12:22–34, we find the familiar passage which advises us to avoid worrying about the necessities of life.

(1) The world may run after such things (v 30), but the disciple cannot.

(2) Provide treasures in heaven by selling possessions and giving to the poor (v 33).

(3) A powerful lesson is found in v 34, namely that we can put our money in the right place as a means of getting our hearts in the right place.

g. In 14:12–14, Jesus tells us to focus on giving to those

who cannot pay us back in any way.

h. In 14:33, we are told that we cannot be disciples unless we give up all of our possessions (NASV).

i. In 16:1-15, Jesus gives us the Parable of the Shrewd Manager and makes some of the most abrupt comments about money anywhere in the Bible.

   (1) Going to heaven is clearly related to our use of worldly wealth (vv 9-12).

   (2) In order to love God, we must *hate* and *despise* materialism (v 13).

   (3) The Pharisees loved money, which was *detestable* in the sight of God (vv 14-15).

j. In 18:18-27, the Rich Young Ruler discovered that all of his religiosity could not offset his love for possessions.

   (1) Because his love for money blocked Jesus from being Lord in his life, he was commanded to sell *everything* he owned and give all of it to the poor (v 22).

   (2) After his refusal, Jesus replied that it was very hard for the rich to enter the kingdom (vv 23-24).

k. In 19:1-9, Zacchaeus was used as an example of someone who, after repentance, viewed and used money rightly.

   (1) On the spot, he vowed to give a half of his possessions to the poor (a tithe, plus special contributions would have been no problem to him).

   (2) He then offered to go far beyond the call of duty in making any former misdealing right. Once a person sees Jesus like he did, possessions drop *way down* on the priority list!

l. In 21:1-4, the widow who gave her last two coins was

used as an example of true sacrificial giving.

(1) What we have left after giving is far more a barometer of our hearts than the amount that we actually give.

(2) From man's viewpoint, she did a foolish thing, but Jesus was quite happy about it.

(3) Keep in mind that she was giving outwardly to a fairly corrupt religious system, but Jesus saw her gift as one totally given to God.

B. Practical impact on relationships

1. Someone said that the tragedy of our day is that we love things and use people, rather than *loving* people and *using* things.

2. Loving things has a huge impact on our relationships in a number of ways.

   a. We may spend too much time trying to make money to *buy* more possessions, and we often spend too much time *thinking* about them.

   b. Our misconceptions about what will make us happy interfere with the focus we need to have on other people. ("If I just had _____, then I would be happy." That kind of thinking is Satan's lie.)

   c. One of the worst things about possessions is that they quickly begin to possess *us*! They must be fixed, cleaned, painted, mowed, swept, upgraded, serviced, etc., etc.! The time spent in these ways can be staggering, if we allow it to be.

3. Materialism is not easy to define. Most of us define it as what the person just above our income or standard of living has. How can we tell if we are guilty of it or not?

   a. Is giving at least a tenth of your gross income a

challenge to your heart?

b. How about giving for special contributions—it is a *duty* or a delight?

c. Do you have problems with envy toward those who have more than you?

d. Do you find yourself mistrusting church leaders regarding how the money that we give to God is spent?

e. Are you *anxious* when children or others may be a threat to your possessions?

f. What do you possess right now that would be very difficult to part with?

g. Where would you *not* be willing to move, or how would you not be willing to live? The Rich Young Ruler drew a line through the middle of his life and was willing to put everything over the line for God—except for *one thing!* Do you have such a *one thing* in your life?

III. Worldliness Through Selfishness

A. Biblical teaching

1. In Romans 1, the focus on *self* was precisely the reason most of these sins became so entrenched in the lives of the people being described.

2. In 2 Timothy 3, the case is the same, but here Paul mentions specifically that the people were *"lovers of themselves"* (v 2).

3. Selfishness is one of the most pervasive sins with which any of us deals. For this reason, Jesus started with the command to *deny self* (Luke 9:23).

4. Since the sin is so obvious, there is no need to multiply the many scriptures which relate to the subject. Therefore, we

will deal with the ways in which this sin makes itself seen in our lives.

B. Types of selfish sins

1. Self-gratification

    a. Living by pleasure instead of by principle.

    b. Doing what feels good at the moment—the devil's plan is much like our modern credit system: Buy now and pay later. (With Satan, we enjoy the quick pleasures of sin but the interest paid in heartaches lasts a long time. God's plan is to pay up front with righteousness and discipline and then to enjoy tremendous dividends for a long time.)

    c. This approach makes us undisciplined, unorganized, unproductive, unfaithful, and certainly unfulfilled.

2. Self-justification

    a. We rationalize our problems and sins instead of accepting 100% responsibility for what we have done and who we really are.

    b. We blame our background, our families, our circumstances, and maybe even our discipler.

    c. Yet, we are who we are because ultimately we have *chosen* it!

3. Self-consciousness

    a. This *self* sin makes us very focused on what others may be thinking about us. We may imagine that people are looking at us and talking about us. We can become paranoid, believing that we are not liked and that others are even out to get us.

    b. We are afraid of people, and Satan uses our cowardice to kill our evangelism.

    c. We are insecure, which is a sin because we are centered

on ourselves rather than on God.

4. Self-will

   a. The self-willed person rebels against authority, does not like seeking and following advice, and filters the directions he does receive.

   b. This sin pushes us toward comfort, materialism and greed. Therefore, when the way is too difficult, it is much easier to give up and give in.

5. Self-pity

   a. This person feels sorry for himself and works hard to evoke the same feelings in others toward him.

   b. Pity parties are commonplace, as are depression, bitterness, sarcasm and cynicism.

   c. Past hurts are magnified and massaged, as an unforgiving spirit grows stronger.

   d. Self-protectiveness blocks a giving away of the heart and the closeness of relationships which that produces.

C. Practical impact on relationships

1. Not much explanation is needed in this area either, because relationships are all about giving and not about getting.

2. The words of Philippians 2:1-11 are very appropriate for us in learning to refuse selfishness and to accept our responsibility to love as Jesus loved with an unconditional commitment to the good of others no matter what.

3. Self-denial is the answer to all these sins of *self*, which means that we deny our selfish *feelings* in order to do the right things for others, just as Jesus did in the Garden of Gethsemane.

IV. Worldliness Through Pride

A. Biblical teaching

1. As in the case of selfishness, many of the sins in both Romans 1 and 2 Timothy 3 have their roots in pride. Unlike selfishness, pride is not always so obvious.

2. There are many types of pride and many manifestations of it in the ways we view ourselves and others. A look at these and the scriptures that relate to them will be helpful at this point.

3. **Types** of pride

   a. Intellect—1 Corinthians 1:19–29; Romans 1:22

   b. Possessions—1 Timothy 6:7–10

   c. Appearance—1 Timothy 2:9–10

   d. Social standing—James 2:1–9

   e. Race—Acts 22:1-22; Romans 2

   f. Spirituality—Luke 18:9–14

   g. Position—Mark 10:35–45

4. **Manifestations** of pride

   a. In the way that we view *ourselves*.

      (1) We want everything our way, because it is always the best.

      (2) We have to have our hand in everything, because no one else can do it quite as well as we can.

      (3) We have to have the last word (or last story).

      (4) We talk too much and listen too little, because our opinions are so important. (We may talk too little for fear that we may come across in the wrong way —this too is pride.)

      (5) We take credit for everything, losing gratitude

toward God and others.

(6) We see the sins of others much better than we see our own sins (or we may be *proud* of our own openness and humility!).

(7) We expect to be a special case, the exception to the rule.

(8) We are anxiety-ridden. If we cannot figure out how to get it done, then surely no one else can, including God himself!

b. In the way that we view *others*

(1) We do not like asking for and following advice. It grates on us to have to be submissive, especially to certain people.

(2) We do not like being corrected, especially in front of others.

(3) We are impatient with others, especially if we do not think that they are as smart as we are.

(4) We manipulate others in order to get our way, because it is obviously the best way.

(5) We often feel superior to others, and if we tend to feel inferior in some way, we find a way to tear them down in our own minds so that we can feel better about ourselves.

(6) We have difficulty admitting our weaknesses and sins and making heartfelt apologies.

(7) We have difficulty admitting our need for others and in expressing our love and appreciation for them verbally.

B. Practical impact on relationships

1. Pride makes others resist us, either outwardly or inwardly.

  a. This resistance may be caused by godliness on the other person's part, because God himself resists those who are proud (1 Peter 5:5).

  b. On the other hand, the resistance may be caused by pride on the other person's part, because pride in one person often brings it out in another person.

  c. Do you feel resistance to prideful people? If so, for which of the above two reasons?

2. Pride keeps us from reaching out to others in order to build relationships.

  a. We are afraid of how we may or may not be accepted by them.

  b. That fear is caused by pride. Our popular word insecurity is a synonym for pride. It is commonly thought that our insecurity causes us to have a sort of defensive pride, a protective reaction. The converse is more likely the case—our pride causes us to be insecure.

3. Pride damages relationships in dozens of ways.

  a. In the NIV, there are 61 references to pride.

  b. In order to get the full impact of the damage that pride causes us and others in our lives, look up these passages and apply them to your life.

  c. As you do it, ask God to help you see yourself as you really are, and then to give you the will and strength to change into a humble person.

LOVE
One
ANOTHER

_____
_____
_____
_____
_____
_____
_____
_____
_____
_____
_____
_____
_____
_____
_____
_____
_____
_____
_____
_____
_____
_____
_____
_____
_____
_____
_____
_____
_____
_____
_____
_____
_____

CHAPTER TWO

LOVE:
Defined by *One Another* Relationships

INTRODUCTION

1. The New Testament is full of passages that regulate the Christian's attitudes and behavior toward others in the body of Christ.

2. These teachings come in many forms, and all of these forms are equally valid and helpful.

3. However, the phrases *one another* and *each other* are found numbers of times in the context of Christian relationships, and in order to narrow down the topic into manageable portions, we are going to examine only the passages that contain these specific phrases.

4. As we will see, the religion of Jesus Christ is definitely a *one another* religion.

5. First, these passages will be written out as they appear chronologically in the New Testament.

6. Second, they will be outlined according to subject into these three categories: the atmosphere of peace; the attitudes of love; and the actions of encouragement.

23

The New Testament Passages in Chronological Order

Mark 9:50—"Salt is good, but if it loses its saltiness, how can you make it salty again? Have salt in yourselves, and be at peace with *each other*."

John 13:34—"A new command I give you: Love *one another*. As I have loved you, so you must love *one another*."

John 13:35—"By this all men will know that you are my disciples, if you love *one another*."

John 15:12—"My command is this: Love *each other* as I have loved you.

John 15:17—"This is my command: Love *each other*."

Romans 12:10—Be devoted to *one another* in brotherly love. Honor one another above yourselves.

Romans 12:16—Live in harmony with *one another*. Do not be proud, but be willing to associate with people of low position. Do not be conceited.

Romans 13:8—Let no debt remain outstanding, except the continuing debt to love *one another*, for he who loves his fellowman has fulfilled the law.

Romans 14:13—Therefore let us stop passing judgment on *one another*. Instead, make up your mind not to put any stumbling block or obstacle in your brother's way.

Romans 15:7—Accept *one another*, then, just as Christ accepted you, in order to bring praise to God.

Romans 15:14—I myself am convinced, my brothers, that you yourselves are full of goodness, complete in knowledge and competent to instruct *one another*.

Romans 16:16—Greet *one another* with a holy kiss. All the churches of Christ send greetings.

1 Corinthians 1:10—I appeal to you, brothers, in the name of our Lord Jesus Christ, that all of you agree with *one another* so that there may be no divisions among you and that you may be perfectly united in mind and thought.

1 Corinthians 7:5—Do not deprive *each other* except by mutual consent and for a time, so that you may devote yourselves to prayer. Then come together again so that Satan will not tempt you because of your lack of self-control.

1 Corinthians 11:33—So then, my brothers, when you come together to eat, wait for *each other*.

1 Corinthians 12:25—so that there should be no division in the body, but that its parts should have equal concern for *each other*.

1 Corinthians 16:20—All the brothers here send you greetings. Greet *one another* with a holy kiss.

2 Corinthians 13:12—Greet *one another* with a holy kiss.

Galatians 5:13—You, my brothers, were called to be free. But do not use your freedom to indulge the sinful nature; rather, serve *one another* in love.

Galatians 5:15—If you keep on biting and devouring each other, watch out or you will be destroyed by *each other*.

Galatians 5:26—Let us not become conceited, provoking and envying *each other*.

Ephesians 4:2—Be completely humble and gentle; be patient, bearing with *one another* in love.

Ephesians 4:32—Be kind and compassionate to *one another*, forgiving *each other*, just as in Christ God forgave you.

Ephesians 5:19—Speak to *one another* with psalms, hymns and spiritual songs. Sing and make music in your heart to the Lord,

Ephesians 5:21—Submit to *one another* out of reverence for Christ.

Philippians 4:2—I plead with Euodia and I plead with Syntyche to agree with *each other* in the Lord.

Colossians 3:9—Do not lie to *each other*, since you have taken off your old self with its practices

Colossians 3:13—Bear with *each other* and forgive whatever grievances you may have against *one another*. Forgive as the Lord forgave you.

Colossians 3:16—Let the word of Christ dwell in you richly as you teach and admonish *one another* with all wisdom, and as you sing psalms, hymns and spiritual songs with gratitude in your hearts to God.

1 Thessalonians 3:12—May the Lord make your love increase and overflow for *each other* and for everyone else, just as ours does for you.

1 Thessalonians 4:9—Now about brotherly love we do not need to write to you, for you yourselves have been taught by God to love *each other*.

1 Thessalonians 4:18—Therefore encourage *each other* with these words.

1 Thessalonians 5:11—Therefore encourage *one another* and build *each other* up, just as in fact you are doing.

1 Thessalonians 5:13—Hold them in the highest regard in love because of their work. Live in peace with *each other*.

1 Thessalonians 5:15—Make sure that nobody pays back wrong for wrong, but always try to be kind to *each other* and to everyone else.

2 Thessalonians 1:3—We ought always to thank God for you, brothers, and rightly so, because your faith is growing more and more, and the love every one of you has for *each other* is increasing.

Hebrews 3:13—But encourage *one another* daily, as long as it is called Today, so that none of you may be hardened by sin's deceitfulness.

**Hebrews 10:24**—And let us consider how we may spur *one another* on toward love and good deeds.

Hebrews 10:25—Let us not give up meeting together, as some are in the habit of doing, but let us encourage *one another*— and all the more as you see the Day approaching.

Hebrews 13:1—Keep on loving *each other* as brothers.

James 4:11—Brothers, do not slander *one another*. Anyone who speaks against his brother or judges him speaks against the law and judges it. When you judge the law, you are not keeping it, but sitting in judgment on it.

James 5:9—Don't grumble against *each other*, brothers, or you will be judged. The Judge is standing at the door!

James 5:16—Therefore confess your sins to *each other* and pray for *each other* so that you may be healed. The prayer of a righteous man is powerful and effective.

1 Peter 1:22—Now that you have purified yourselves by obeying the truth so that you have sincere love for your brothers, love *one another* deeply, from the heart.

1 Peter 3:8—Finally, all of you, live in harmony with one *another*; be sympathetic, love as brothers, be compassionate and humble.

1 Peter 4:8—Above all, love *each other* deeply, because love covers over a multitude of sins.

1 Peter 4:9—Offer hospitality to *one another* without grumbling.

1 Peter 5:5—Young men, in the same way be submissive to those who are older. All of you, clothe yourselves with humility toward *one another*, because, "God opposes the proud but gives grace to the humble."

1 Peter 5:14—Greet *one another* with a kiss of love. Peace to all of you who are in Christ.

1 John 1:7—But if we walk in the light, as he is in the light, we have fellowship with *one another*, and the blood of Jesus, his Son, purifies us from all sin.

1 John 3:11—This is the message you heard from the beginning: We should love *one another*.

1 John 3:23—And this is his command: to believe in the name of his Son, Jesus Christ, and to love *one another* as he commanded us.

1 John 4:7—Dear friends, let us love *one another*, for love comes from God. Everyone who loves has been born of God and knows God.

1 John 4:11—Dear friends, since God so loved us, we also ought to love *one another*.

1 John 4:12—No one has ever seen God; but if we love *one another*, God lives in us and his love is made complete in us.

2 John 1:5—And now, dear lady, I am not writing you a new command but one we have had from the beginning. I ask that we love *one another*.

LOVE
One
ANOTHER

_____
_____
_____
_____
_____
_____
_____
_____
_____
_____
_____
_____
_____
_____
_____
_____
_____
_____
_____
_____
_____
_____
_____
_____
_____
_____
_____
_____
_____
_____

I. The Atmosphere of Peace

A. The Commands

1. Be at peace

    a. Mark 9:50—"Salt is good, but if it loses its saltiness, how can you make it salty again? Have salt in yourselves, and be at peace with *each other*."

    b. 1 Thessalonians 5:13—Hold them in the highest regard in love because of their work. Live in peace with *each other*.

2. Live in harmony

    a. Romans 12:16—Live in harmony with *one another*. Do not be proud, but be willing to associate with people of low position. Do not be conceited.

    b. 1 Peter 3:8—Finally, all of you, live in harmony with *one another*; be sympathetic, love as brothers, be compassionate and humble.

B. The Attitudes

1. Negatives to avoid

    a. Not judgmental: Romans 14:13—Therefore let us stop passing judgment on *one another*. Instead, make up your mind not to put any stumbling block or obstacle in your brother's way.

    b. Not conceited and envious: Galatians 5:26—Let us not become conceited, provoking and envying *each other*.

2. Positives to pursue

    a. Submissiveness: Ephesians 5:21—Submit to *one another* out of reverence for Christ.

    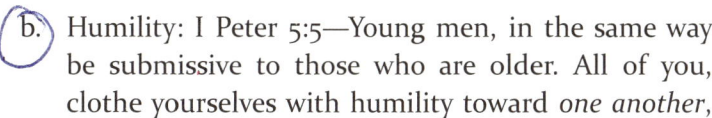
    b. Humility: I Peter 5:5—Young men, in the same way be submissive to those who are older. All of you, clothe yourselves with humility toward *one another*,

because, "God opposes the proud but gives grace to the humble."

C. The Actions

1. Negatives to avoid

   a. No depriving one's mate of the sexual relationship: I Corinthians 7:5—Do not deprive *each other* except by mutual consent and for a time, so that you may devote yourselves to prayer. Then come together again so that Satan will not tempt you because of your lack of self-control.

   b. No destroying of each other: Galatians 5:15—If you keep on biting and devouring *each other*, watch out or you will be destroyed by each other.

   c. No lying: Colossians 3:9—Do not lie to *each other*, since you have taken off your old self with its practices.

   d. No slander and grumbling: James 4:11; 5:9—Brothers, do not slander *one another*. Anyone who speaks against his brother or judges him speaks against the law and judges it. When you judge the law, you are not keeping it, but sitting in judgment on it. / Don't grumble against *each other*, brothers, or you will be judged. The Judge is standing at the door!

2. Positives to pursue

   a. Agree with each other: I Corinthians 1:10; Philippians 4:2—I appeal to you, brothers, in the name of our Lord Jesus Christ, that all of you agree with *one another* so that there may be no divisions among you and that you may be perfectly united in mind and thought. / I plead with Euodia and I plead with Syntyche to agree with *each other* in the Lord.

   b. Bear with each other: Colossians 3:13—Bear with *each*

other and forgive whatever grievances you may have against one another. Forgive as the Lord forgave you.

c. Fellowship with one another: I John 1:7—But if we walk in the light, as he is in the light, we have fellowship with *one another*, and the blood of Jesus, his Son, purifies us from all sin.

II. The Attitudes of Love

A. Love's Commitment

1. Seen in its devotion: Romans 12:10—Be devoted to *one another* in brotherly love. Honor *one another* above yourselves.

2. Seen in its description (from *agape* unless otherwise noted):

   a. The command: John 13:34—"A new command I give you: Love *one another*. As I have loved you, so you must love *one another*." (See also John 15:17; 1 John 3:11, 23; 4:7; 2 John 1:5.)

   b. The extent:

      (1) To increase and overflow: 1 Thessalonians 3:12— May the Lord make your love increase and overflow for *each other* and for everyone else, just as ours does for you. (See also 2 Thessalonians 1:3.)

      (2) To come deeply from the heart: 1 Peter 1:22—Now that you have purified yourselves by obeying the truth so that you have sincere love (*phileo*) for your brothers, love *one another* deeply, from the heart. (See also 1 Peter 4:8.)

   c. The obligation:

      (1) A continuing debt: Romans 13:8—Let no debt remain outstanding, except the continuing debt to love *one another*, for he who loves his fellowman

has fulfilled the law.

(2) As taught by God: 1 Thess. 4:9—Now about brotherly love (*phileo*) we do not need to write to you, for you yourselves have been taught by God to love *each other.*

(3) To keep on loving: Heb. 13:1—Keep on loving (*phileo*) *each other* as brothers.

(4) Because God first loved us: 1 John 4:11—Dear friends, since God so loved us, we also ought to love *one another.*

d. The demonstration:

(1) That we are his disciples: John 13:35—By this all men will know that you are my disciples, if you love *one another.*"

(2) That men might see God in us: 1 John 4:12—No one has ever seen God; but if we love *one another*, God lives in us and his love is made complete in us.

B. Love's Respect

1. Shown by honoring: Romans 12:10—Be devoted to *one another* in brotherly love (*phileo*). Honor *one another* above yourselves.

2. Shown by accepting: Romans 15:7—Accept *one another*, then, just as Christ accepted you, in order to bring praise to God.

3. Shown by equal concern: 1 Corinthians 12:25—So that there should be no division in the body, but that its parts should have equal concern for *each other.*

C. Love's Mercy

1. Shown by compassion: Ephesians 4:32—Be kind and compassionate to *one another*, forgiving *each other*, just as in

Christ God forgave you.

2. Shown by kindness: 1 Thessalonians 5:15—Make sure that nobody pays back wrong for wrong, but always try to be kind to each other and to everyone else. (See also Ephesians 4:32.)

3. Shown by forgiveness: Colossians 3:13—Bear with each other and forgive whatever grievances you may have against one another. Forgive as the Lord forgave you. (See also Ephesians 4:32.)

III. The Actions of Encouragement

A. Instructing One Another

1. Competency to counsel: Romans 15:14—I myself am convinced, my brothers, that you yourselves are full of goodness, complete in knowledge and competent to instruct *one another*.

2. Communicated in singing: Ephesians 5:19—Speak to *one another* with psalms, hymns and spiritual songs. Sing and make music in your heart to the Lord,

3. Carried out in wisdom given by God: Colossians 3:16—Let the word of Christ dwell in you richly as you teach and admonish *one another* with all wisdom, and as you sing psalms, hymns and spiritual songs with gratitude in your hearts to God.

B. Serving One Another

1. Freedom to serve: Galatians 5:13—You, my brothers, were called to be free. But do not use your freedom to indulge the sinful nature; rather, serve *one another* in love.

2. In hospitality

    a. By waiting and sharing: 1 Corinthians 11:33—So then,

my brothers, when you come together to eat, wait for *each other.*

b. Without grumbling: 1 Peter 4:9—Offer hospitality to *one another* without grumbling.

C. Encouraging One Another

1. The specific commands for it

   a. Use God's promises: 1 Thessalonians 4:18—Therefore encourage *each other* with these words.

   b. Build up one another: 1 Thessalonians 5:11—Therefore encourage *one another* and build *each other* up, just as in fact you are doing.

   c. Make it daily: Hebrews 3:13—But encourage *one another* daily, as long as it is called Today, so that none of you may be hardened by sin's deceitfulness.

   d. Encourage to give up no meetings: Hebrews 10:25— Let us not give up meeting together, as some are in the habit of doing, but let us encourage *one another*—and all the more as you see the Day approaching.

2. The warmth in it, Romans 16:16—Greet *one another* with a holy kiss. All the churches of Christ send greetings. (See also 1 Corinthians 16:20; 2 Corinthians 13:12; 1 Peter 5:14.)

3. The challenge of it, Hebrews 10:24—And let us consider how we may spur *one another* on toward love and good deeds.

4. The healing from it, James 5:16—Therefore confess your sins to *each other* and pray for each other so that you may be healed. The prayer of a righteous man is powerful and effective.

OBSERVATIONS ABOUT PEACE

1. Peace with others grows out of having peace with God. When we really feel that peace with him, we are much more likely to feel at peace with others. Therefore, when we feel anxious with others, we need to start with an examination of how we are feeling about our relationship with God.

2. Maintaining peace is much more than the absence of outward conflict, as the world normally defines it. Peace between disciples is a harmony of the hearts.

3. The Scriptures are very clear about the destructive power of envy, gossip and slander. These sins arise out of a competitive spirit which is fed by a negative view of oneself. Being *discerning* about another person means that we are committed to helping them deal with their weaknesses. Being *critical* puts us in the judge's seat with little or no intention of actually helping the person to change.

4. Along these lines, some feel that they are being merely observant about another person when they are actually practicing the deadly art of *objective negativity,* This deceptive approach begins with the positives about someone, interjects a *but,* and then proceeds to discount the positives by leaving the negatives as the last thing to enter the memory banks.

OBSERVATIONS ABOUT LOVE

1. The *new* command of John 13:34 is not new in some ways, because the whole Old Testament was based on the need to love God and neighbor (Matthew 22:36-40). However, the love for others was defined by the phrase *as you love yourself.* The measure of the love in this new command was *as I have loved you.* Another aspect of the newness was in its design to convince others that we are disciples of Christ, and thereby help them to be drawn to him. It is to be an evangelistic love. Finally, the love was new in that it operated among disciples who were bound together by the blood of Christ. No physical relatives could ever be as

close in heart and purpose as *blood* relatives in Christ!

2. Love in the world is a *because of* type of love. Love in the Kingdom is an *in spite of* type of love. In other words, we don't love because of any benefits that come our way (though we should appreciate them). We love in order to be a blessing to the other person no matter the sacrifice or the difficulty involved.

3. To whom do you show the most love? To the ones you claim to love the most, such as your mate or roommates? Truthfully, we often let down our guards with the ones we are around the most and treat them the worst.

4. 1 Peter 1:22 contains some powerful truths about love. One, we must be forgiven to truly practice sincere love (that is, with no ulterior motives). Two, we begin with the friendship type of love (*phileo*), but then move to the deeper type (*agape*). Three, this godly type of love is not only active good will or unconditionally seeking the good of another—it must be full of heartfelt emotions.

5. According to 1 Thessalonians 3:12, our love is to increase and overflow. Therefore, it is a very *inclusive* love and not an *exclusive* type; limitless and not limited in scope. The worldly concept is to love only a few in a really special way. Not surprisingly, jealousy comes into play rather easily due to possessiveness. On the other hand, when we love like God, we can love more and more people more and more deeply. And we rejoice when our closest brothers and sisters get much closer to others besides us!

OBSERVATIONS ABOUT ENCOURAGEMENT

1. We are, according to Romans 15:14, competent to instruct (*counsel* is the idea) one another. As grateful as I am for Christian psychologists and psychiatrists in the Body, I am convinced that we have swung too far in the direction of thinking that we cannot counsel one another. Although some do need professional counseling, many are dodging discipleship by claiming to have deeper problems that can be helped by only a select few. Do you

really think that Bible-believing people throughout the centuries had to languish through life without being able to change because counseling professionals had not appeared on the scene yet? Psychology in general has but one major contribution to make—that of *diagnosis*. Knowing where you got your hang-ups does little to change them. Biblical repentance and the power of God are the prescription for the changes we need to make and can make! No amount of counseling will ever substitute for those things.

2.   According to Hebrews 10:24, we need encouragement to love the way we should. The reverse of that is also true—we need love in order to give and receive the encouragement in the best way. When the relationships are tight, encouragement can be very challenging and yet highly appreciated. When the relationships are not sensed as being from the heart (with emotions involved), challenges are much more difficult to take and appreciate.

3.   The whole picture of encouragement includes everything we need to be like Jesus. Some see it as being only positive. They would prefer be told that they are fine the way they are, rather than be challenged to be more like Jesus. As time goes by, friends who are conflict avoiders with us will be less and less appreciated if we have a heart to grow spiritually. The ones whom we will look back on with fonder memories will be those who encouraged us with both positives and negatives about ourselves.

4.   The encouragement we are able to receive is tied rather closely to the openness that we bring into the relationship. The more vulnerable we are with *who* we really are, the more we can be seriously encouraged. Encouragement, like love, must be based in truth to have the desired effect on us. Being open with another person is one of the greatest gifts we can offer. Nothing is more special than another allowing you into the feeling level of his or her life. Anyone in the world can talk about things, places and people. Only those who are committed to love and encouragement can take off the protective masks and share heart to heart.

LOVE
One
ANOTHER

_____
_____
_____
_____
_____
_____
_____
_____
_____
_____
_____
_____
_____
_____
_____
_____
_____
_____
_____
_____
_____
_____
_____
_____
_____
_____
_____
_____
_____
_____

CHAPTER THREE

LOVE:
Distilled by Discipling Relationships

INTRODUCTION

1. Discipleship is a basic component of Christianity. The deadness and ineffectiveness of modern churches can be traced *directly* to a lack of discipleship.

2. Discipleship has a *vertical* aspect and a *horizontal* aspect. The vertical has to do with our relationship to Christ, which must be based on our total commitment to him. The horizontal aspect has to do with our relationship to one another as fellow disciples in his family.

3. For our purposes in this present series, we are going to concentrate on the relationships in the church, especially on what we call *discipling relationships*. (Such terms are a matter of choice and expediency, but they do help us communicate effectively.) However, these relationships can work *only* if the total commitment to following Christ as Lord is present to begin with!

4. The one another/each other passages make it clear that we all have some responsibility to everyone else in the church. But it should be obvious that more specific responsibilities within certain relationships

are necessary if we are going to keep growing spiritually and accomplish the mission Christ has for his kingdom on the earth.

5. As the old saying goes, "Everybody's business is no-body's business"!

6. Therefore, we must understand both the biblical basis for discipling relationships and the practicals needed in order to make them effective.

I. The Biblical Basis for Discipling Relationships

A. Jesus and his levels of relationships, a key observation

1. Jesus related to those he was trying to influence on a number of different size levels. Going from the larger to the smaller, he taught the crowds; he met with 500 in Galilee by appointment after his resurrection (1 Corinthians 15:6; Matthew 28:7–10); he had the 120 in Jerusalem when the church was established (Acts 1); he had a group of 72 which he sent out on a preaching tour (Luke 10); he had the 12 apostles; then the three within the 12—Peter, James and John—and a special individual relationship with John, the beloved disciple, as well as with most or all of the other apostles.

2. It is an interesting exercise to apply each of the levels to our situation today. Each must have had some purpose in the discipleship plan of Jesus.

3. However, it should be obvious that the smaller the group size, the more impacting it would be on an individual.

4. Therefore, we definitely need to concentrate on the smaller settings, for they are the most helpful in prompting

people to change into being more like Jesus.

B. Jesus and the Great Commission, a key passage—Matthew 28:19–20

> *"Therefore go and make disciples of all nations, baptizing them in the name of the Father and of the Son and of the Holy Spirit, and teaching them to obey everything I have commanded you. And surely I am with you always, to the very end of the age."*

Several foundational lessons are contained in this great commission:

1. We are to make *disciples*—not simply church members, religious people, or nicer persons.

    a. Before any person is a biblical candidate for baptism, they must have made the *decision* to be a disciple, and they must have learned enough of what this means to make an *educated* decision.

    b. This decision is called *repentance* in Acts 2:38.

        (1) To properly understand repentance, you have to properly understand *sin*.

        (2) Sin, from the Greek word *hamartia*, is derived from an archery term, meaning to *miss the mark*.

        (3) Since our mark is being like Jesus (1 John 2:6), it should be obvious that the mark can be missed by *doing* things that he would *not* do, or by *not doing* things that he *would* do. Whichever way one misses the mark, he still misses the mark!

        (4) Therefore, repentance is making the firm decision to stop doing wrong things and to start doing right things. Most religious people focus only on the first part of repentance and not the last part. In this case, their repentance is not true biblical repentance.

A
t one point in my life, after learning about discipleship, I preached and taught much about our responsibilities as disciples in the traditional type church for which I was serving as a minister. For a long time, the reluctance of the members to put into practice the things I was teaching was a mystery to me. Finally, it dawned on me that they had originally been baptized for different reasons than to be disciples! They had missed the teaching of Matthew 28 by a long shot and not signed up for a commitment which was that serious! The only conclusion that I could reach regarding them was that they had not biblically repented and therefore were not really disciples.

2. We are to *baptize* them—with the *one* baptism of Ephesians 4:5.

   a. This baptism *in form* is a burial in water (Acts 8:34–39; Romans 6:3–4).

   b. This baptism *in intent* is a decision to be a disciple in all of the ways described in the New Testament.

   c. It should be rather obvious that no one can be biblically baptized until they are old enough to make such a decision and then follow through with it.

3. We are to *teach* them (the baptized ones) to *obey everything* that Jesus commanded the apostles.

   a. Just like every child born into a family has to be trained, every child in God's family must be trained.

   b. We are not simply to *teach* everything Jesus commanded, but to teach to *obey*. (Consider this difference in the rearing of children—it is a very *large* difference!) This directive of Jesus can only be carried out when someone is directly responsible for the training in every disciple's life.

c.   Just attending church could not possibly accomplish what is being commanded here—it takes a *specific* person to train another specific person in the *specific* commands of Jesus.

d.   Another vital point in this text concerns the standards of being a disciple. Our standard is Jesus himself (1 John 2:6), and this standard is for every disciple. No person in the church is to have more commitment to Jesus and his cause than any other person. We are to obey *everything*!

4.   This passage deals with a basic principle of learning used in all of life.

a.   Most of what we learn in life is learned in exactly this manner—it is learning by doing, on-the-job training, and an apprenticeship approach to life.

b.   The Bible contains very few specifics about some highly important areas of life—prayer, evangelism, family life, etc.

c.   The absence of more specifics in such vital areas demonstrates very clearly that God intends the discipling relationships to fill in the gaps as we learn to be like Jesus.

d.   Actually, the *one another* responsibilities are carried out in a number of ways—within general relationships in the church, discipleship groups of one kind or another, and physical families of disciples, as well as in discipleship partner relationships.

e.   But the discipleship partner arrangement is the most effective way to obey the injunctions of Matthew 28 and the natural outgrowth of evangelism. When you initially study with a person to help them reach the point of baptism, it will seem obvious that the relationship should continue as you strive to help them mature.

C. Jesus and his use of group discipling, a key concept

1. Group discipling was used quite often by Jesus, no doubt for a number of reasons.

    a. Relating to one's discipler is one thing, but relating to one's peers is yet another—discipleship groups reveal some things about our characters that may not be revealed any other way.

    b. Also, the group dynamic enables everyone to help and be helped in a powerful way.

    c. The *think tank* setting spawns ideas that will help everyone to be more effective as disciples.

    d. Finally, Jesus was able to simply save time in his training of these men by giving his more general directions only once. (He did use individual times for meeting more *specific* needs—for example in John 21 with Peter.)

2. The book of Mark contains some very helpful examples of group discipling times:

    a. Mark 7:14–23—After Jesus had taught the crowds, he then answered questions from the disciples in a more private setting.

    b. Mark 8:27–33—Jesus rebuked Peter in the group, and then went on to teach on the same subject to the crowds.

    c. Mark 9:14–32

    (1) After casting a demon out of the boy, he answered the disciples' questions regarding their failure to accomplish the task.

    (2) Evidently because of the importance of the issues

being taught, Jesus took them away from the possibility of interruptions to continue the teaching.

d. Mark 9:33–37—In this setting, he used an object lesson, a little child, to teach them about humility.

e. Mark 10:35–45

(1) Notice the atmosphere Jesus had created among them—James and John were open about their ambitions.

(2) After the others became jealous and prideful, Jesus called them together to teach on humility and servant leadership.

f. Mark 12:41–44—After seeing the widow's financial sacrifice, Jesus called his disciples to him to teach them about real giving in the sight of God.

II. The Powerful Purpose for Discipling Relationships

A. To form Christ in another person—Galatians 4:19

1. This task is not an easy one and cannot be accomplished without some labors and struggles (Colossians 1:28–29).

2. The maturing process being described is what Jesus referred to in Matthew 28:19 (teaching the baptized disciples to obey everything) and in John 15:16 (bearing fruit that will last).

3. Once we have discipled someone *to* Jesus (conversion), then we must disciple them *into* the *image* of Jesus (maturation)!

4. This process takes into consideration the needs of the whole person—their physical, emotional and spiritual needs. As we will see shortly, the overall focus of any disciple's life is to seek and save the lost, but only healthy, growing disciples can effectively do this task.

B. **To accomplish the mission of Jesus**—Matthew 28:18–20

1. If Christ is truly formed in another person, that person will have the same focus in life which Jesus himself had (Luke 19:10).

2. Therefore, the discipling relationship will address all areas of life, because all areas are related either directly or indirectly to evangelism.

   a. A person's personality, mannerisms, speech patterns and even dress tie in to his effectiveness in influencing others for Christ. Therefore, at least some attention should be given to them as a part of the discipling relationship.

   b. The practicals about how to share our faith, follow-up with those whom we are trying to influence, setup and teach studies, and disciple others are all a part of what is needed in discipling someone to focus on the mission of Jesus.

III. The Healthy Heart in Discipling Relationships

A. **In order for discipling relationships to work, our hearts must be open to change and eager to change.**

1. Discipling necessarily deals with the outward actions of a disciple, but not without the involvement of the heart.

2. One can do the deeds of a disciple without the heart of a disciple, but if one has the heart of a disciple, he will do the deeds of a disciple.

3. For this reason, Jesus always discipled from the inside out rather than from the outside in.

B. **What are the heart qualities needed by us as disciples?**

1. A *teachable* heart

   a. A teachable heart is shown by *initiation*.

      (1) If our desire is to be as much like Jesus as possible, we will be anxious to ask for input into our lives.

      (2) The early church was together *daily* (Acts 2:46), and we are told to encourage each other *daily* (Hebrews 3:13). Therefore, the disciple should have the desire to be discipled on a *daily* basis.

  b. A teachable heart is shown by *imitation*.

      (1) The principle of imitation is a very practical and very biblical principle.

      (2) On the practical side, we learn most of what we learn in this manner. As others *demonstrate*, we *imitate*!

      (3) On the biblical side, the need for imitation is clear —1 Corinthians 4:14–17; 11:1; Hebrews 13:7.

      (4) The things in another's life that are to be imitated are the Christlike qualities and the effective approaches for serving Christ. Obviously, we are not concerned with imitating incidentals, such as personal preferences, nor are we to imitate weaknesses. But imitation is without doubt the fastest way to grow, and growth is our goal as disciples.

      (5) If imitation seems negative to you, the reason is most likely *pride*—think about it!

2. A *trusting* heart

  a. A trusting heart begins with a complete trust in God, which makes possible the trusting of those people he puts into your life.

  b. The idea that you can trust God without trusting the people he puts in your life is an unbiblical idea and an ungodly idea.

  c. If disciples are to be known by their love (John 13:34–

35), and if love always trusts (1 Corinthians 13:7), then we cannot be disciples without trusting others in the family of God!

3. A *transparent* heart

    a. A transparent heart is open in every area of life because every area of life is to become like Jesus.

    b. James 5:16 tells us that we are to confess our sins to each other. (In the original language, the idea is to be in the *habit* of confessing sins—instead of waiting until you are sick and scared!)

    c. A real disciple is anxious to confess at the temptation level, before sin enters the picture. Playing Battleship Discipleship—waiting for someone to probe out your sins by the hit-or-miss method—is a far cry from having a transparent heart.

    d. Honesty is the key here, in both content and intensity. We should be open with *what* we feel and with how *strongly* we feel it.

4. A *tough* heart

    a. A tough heart stands ready to be challenged to change.

    b. Obviously, all of us have a long way to go in being like Jesus. The only way we are going to change significantly and quickly is to be challenged.

    c. *Comfort zone Christianity* is a denominational concept and totally foreign to the Bible. However, our natural tendency is to want such an approach, and thus our desire to change must be strong enough to offset this tendency.

    d. Our attitude should be that of the psalmist, who wrote: "Let a righteous man strike me—it is a kindness; let him rebuke me—it is oil on my head. My head will not refuse it" (Psalms 141:5). See also Proverbs 27:5–6,17 for similar ideas.

LOVE
One
ANOTHER

_____
_____
_____
_____
_____
_____
_____
_____
_____
_____
_____
_____
_____
_____
_____
_____
_____
_____
_____
_____
_____
_____
_____
_____
_____
_____
_____
_____
_____
_____
_____
_____
_____
_____

IV. The Priceless Practicals in Discipling Relationships

A. Keep the focus *relational* in nature.

1. Discipling relationships are *friendship* focused and not authority focused.

   a. In the next chapter, we will be discussing leader/follower relationships. These relationships are based on *roles* as designated leaders over groups.

   b. Discipling relationships are patterned after family relationships in which older siblings help in the training of their younger siblings.

      (1) The difference in maturity determines the ordering of the relationship.

      (2) Even in the situation where one person is much more mature than the other, the less mature should always feel free to offer input into the life of the more mature person.

      (3) If the less mature one feels intimidated by doing such, or if the more mature one is in any way offended by receiving it, something is wrong with the relationship!

      (4) In the situation with church-supported ministry staff, the relationship in some ways may resemble an employer/employee relationship, but even here, the sense of friendship should predominate.

2. Discipling relationships should provide examples of spiritual best friends, who love unconditionally and unselfishly, seeking only the best interests of the other person.

B. Keep the focus *manageable* in number.

1. Although Jesus worked with people on all different levels, he focused on a *few* whom he poured his life into.

2. In our situations, our schedules will dictate how many we can realistically disciple at any one time.

C. Keep the focus *realistic* in expectations.

1. We must be realistic in what we expect from a discipleship partner, as it relates to time together and to what changes they can help us make. (No matter what else may be said, we are always responsible for our own sins and our own growth.)

2. We must also be realistic in our view of *changes* of discipleship partners.

   a. Some of us are far too unsettled or hurt when such changes occur, and we then are very reluctant to give our hearts to the next discipleship partner we have.

   b. We need a more informed, more realistic, more mature view of these changes.

      (1) Such changes are inevitable if we have a growing church, region or bible talk. At the bible talk level, if we are growing then we will end up as two bible talks. Therefore, changes in discipleship partners are necessary and desirable. If we love the mission, we will be excited about the changes it brings about!

      (2) The worldly view of love is that we can only love a *few* in a really special way. The godly view is that the more *deeply* we love *more and more* people, the more we become like God.

      (3) Although I really miss the time together with former discipleship partners, my life is richer, my heart is larger and more loving, and my anticipation of heaven is keener because of these relationships. In a very real sense, I would have been robbed if changes had not occurred.

(4) Therefore, let's deal with our selfishness, our lack of kingdom focus, and our immaturity. Accept change as from God, and keep giving your heart away to every new discipling relationship you may have. It is the plan of God!

D. Keep the focus *consistent* in schedule.

1. It takes time and scheduling to develop great discipling relationships.

   a. Jesus called his disciples to be with him (Mark 3:14).

   b. Daily contact is more than a good idea—it is in the bible (Hebrews 3:13). We are in the world all day, which takes courage out of us. Thus we need a brother or sister to put courage back *in* (encourage) us daily!

   c. A weekly time together for a couple of hours is a reasonable expectation for all of us—a minimum actually.

2. It takes a scheduled format for impactful weekly discipleship times. Such times should include:

   a. Sharing victories, struggles, sins, dreams, plans and anything else on our hearts about our lives as disciples.

   b. Opening the Bible for insights and answers to the above needs. The sharing of exciting quiet times is another good reason to open the Word together.

   c. Praying together is a constant need—looking for answers without it is to admit a humanistic outlook on life (even life in the Kingdom)!

   d. Asking advice in many areas is vital. We should be tired of making mistakes by now and want to get the best input possible on a consistent basis. "The way of a fool seems right to him, but a wise man listens to advice" (Proverbs 12:15).

e. Getting direction for the upcoming week in the mission (and in related areas) and giving some loving accountability about the directions we received the past week (Luke 9:10). (**Note:** accountability is never designed to make us do something we do not want to do. It is always designed to help us follow through on our good intentions for Jesus. Obviously, if we don't want to be doing what Jesus would do, our intentions are not good!)

Thoughts About Confidentiality

Looking at things from the standpoint of *leadership*, the area of confidentiality is quite involved from a *legal* perspective. Laws are not only quite specific in this area; they are also quite varied from state to state. Such laws do apply to leaders within all types of organizations, whether religious or business. Therefore, the scope and purpose of our study is not such that we should or could deal with this particular topic from the standpoint of *leadership* and *legalities*.

However, considering our biblical responsibilities as *individual* disciples some basic observations would certainly be in order. Sharing something about one person with another person, whether the information falls into the area of confidentiality or not, should always be done with care and consideration. A good place to begin is with the Golden Rule—if the situation were reversed, would you want the same things said about you?

The biblical admonitions that forbid *gossip* and *slander* clearly come into focus at this point. In Proverbs 11:13 a *gossip* is defined as one who betrays a confidence. The *intent* of the one talking is not at issue in the passage—only the *result* is! In Ephesians 4:29, all unwholesome talk is forbidden and is then contrasted with talk that is helpful for building others up and for benefitting those who listen. In 1 Peter 2:1 *every kind* of slander is forbidden. If you are not sure if something is slander or not, assume that it has that potential and take the cautious route. Apply the Golden Rule and the principles of these two passages to help you decide.

If you are thinking about sharing details about another person's life in a potentially sensitive area without their knowledge, ask yourself the following questions:

1. *Why* are you thinking about sharing these things?

2. Will your sharing benefit the one you are sharing about?

3. Will your sharing benefit the one with whom you are sharing?

4. In the reverse situation, would you want the same things shared about you?

As we grow as Christians, we understand more about the grace and forgiveness of God and are much less self-conscious about our weaknesses. I have often said that it is a great comfort to know that I could not be blackmailed in any way regarding my past, because I have been very open publicly about it. Since Satan works best in the dark (John 3:19-21), being open with our sins is a major way to keep him from controlling us. That is why James 5:16 is in the Bible. Therefore, all of us as disciples need to cultivate openness about our own lives and to eliminate the pride which produces self-consciousness. However, our openness about *another's* life is a different issue and needs to be handled with the care discussed above. When you do feel that a third party is needed to assist with some problem, you should get permission of the person you are discipling before talking with that other person.

One final observation is needed on the subject. When sin in a disciple's life has become such that church discipline has to be exercised, the person (and at least the *general nature* of his sin) will be made public within the group with whom they are most closely associated. In the event that someone has become a public enemy of the church, the church must be publicly warned for their own spiritual protection. Along these lines, consider the mention of a number of such enemies *by name* in the New Testament (1 Timothy 1:20; 2 Timothy 1:15; 2:17; 4:10;,14; 3 John 9-10).

Once again, as in all other areas of life the greatest rule is the one Jesus gave in Luke 3:21, *"Do to others as you would have them do to you."*

CHAPTER FOUR

LOVE:
Directed by Leader/Follower Relationships

INTRODUCTION

1. We live in a country that cries out for leadership, but then attempts to *destroy* it because it never measures up to the expectations of the followers.

2. Nothing is more vital to the kingdom of God than having the right kind of leadership and the right kind of followership.

3. Because all of us come out of a confused and sinful world into the kingdom, we almost always bring many misconceptions about leaders and followers with us.

4. Therefore, the goal of this lesson is to help all of us learn how to view and how to function in them in the various roles of leading and following.

5. One key issue in this consideration revolves around the question of authority in the kingdom of God. Because this topic is so very vital, an entire in-depth study is included at the end of this book as an appendix. (This study was first printed as a part of the *Refined by Fire* study on the books of 1 & 2 Peter.)

6. If we replace worldly concepts of leadership and followership with godly ones, we will all say: "'When the princes in Israel take the lead, when the people willingly offer themselves—praise the Lord (Judges 5:2)!

I. The Design for Leadership

A. Leadership is to *meet the needs* of the people.

1. Not every want will be fulfilled, but the genuine needs of those being led should be satisfied.

2. Exodus 18:13–26 describes a key principle, sometimes called the *Jethro Principle*, of how individual needs within even large groups can be met.

   a. One, the larger groups must be broken down into smaller groups with each of these having a leader.

   b. Two, the leaders on these various levels must be responsible for meeting the majority of needs within their groups.

   c. Three, difficult cases can be brought to those who lead on higher levels.

   d. Then, and only then, will leadership be able to stand the strain and the people go home satisfied (v 23—see also Judges 5:2).

   e. However, for this principle to work, the leaders must accept responsibility for their groups, and the people must follow them, respecting the organizational structure and thereby being content with *their* leader.

B. Leadership is to *protect the lives* of the people.

1. A leader is a shepherd, and a shepherd feeds and protects his sheep.

a. See the example of Jesus as the Good Shepherd in John 10).

b. The flock must be protected from the ever-present wolves who show up at the wrong times in the wrong places (Acts 20:28–31).

2. A shepherd/leader is concerned about every aspect in the life of his charges, because he is not just doing a job—he really *cares* (and the sheep always *know* whether he does or not).

C. Leadership is to *train and mature* the hearts of the people.

1. Ephesians 4:11-16 provides a very clear outline of this vital function.

    a. Leaders are to prepare God's people for works of service (some versions have *ministry* instead of service).

    b. It has never been the design of God for leaders to do the work *for* people, but rather to train them and then to all do the work *together*.

2. The denominational approach is the very opposite, taking the approach that someone else can be hired or enrolled to do the work of another.

3. Leaders have work to do as *leaders*, but they also have work to do as individual *disciples*.

    a. When leaders are so busy doing leadership tasks that they have no time to do the things that all disciples should be doing, everyone will be hurt in the long run.

    b. And when leaders do the work that others should be doing, it is not right before God (Acts 6:1–6), and once again, everyone will ultimately be hurt.

II. Motivation by Leadership

A. Motivate through *righteousness*.

1. As leaders on any level, righteousness must characterize our lives and our leadership.

2. Some of Jesus' strongest condemnations were aimed at leaders who were unrighteous and led others unrighteously.

3. In Matthew 23, the unrighteousness of such leaders was described in detail. Looking at the qualities that are the very opposite of the ones described makes for some good insights into what Jesus considered *righteous leadership*.

   a. Practice what you preach (vv 1–4).

   (1) It is significant that Jesus began with the hypocrisy of demanding of others what we are not ourselves doing, or at least really trying hard to do.

   (2) R. L. Whiteside, an old preacher from a former generation said, "I have no respect for a preacher who does not preach better than he lives, nor do I have any respect for one who is not striving to live as well as he preaches!" What he said of preachers applies well to any type of leader.

   b. Serve without concern for recognition (vv 5–12).

   (1) The question of *why* we lead is a much more important question than that of *how* we lead!

   (2) A desire to be noticed, recognized and commended as a leader usually springs from our pride and insecurity.

   (3) On the other hand, when our motivations are righteous, the rewards are many (see vv 11–12).

   c. Convert people to Jesus (vv 13–15).

(1) Jesus was not critical of converting people—that was his heart's desire for the world and the basis of the Great Commission.

(2) He was critical of converting people to *ourselves* (v 15). To the extent that we really ground people in love for Jesus and in loyalty to him, to that extent they will remain faithful.

d. Show integrity in your words (vv 16–22).

(1) No false impressions in trying to make yourself look good.

(2) No promises without following through on them —do what you say you are going to do.

e. Deal with the heart (vv 23–32).

(1) Begin with your own—the issue is not outward appearance but inward attitudes. What do your people *see* in you, and more importantly, what do they *sense* in you?

(2) Then learn to expose and heal the hearts of those whom you lead. If the heart is deceitful above all things (Jeremiah 17:9–10), it will need divine help to change, but God wants to use you as a tool to effect this change.

B. Motivate through *relationship*.

1. The vital distinction between worldly leadership and spiritual leadership concerns the ingredient of relationship.

a. Leaders in the world function mostly out of *position*, whereas leaders in the kingdom function mostly out of *relationship*.

b. In Matthew 20:25–28, Jesus discusses this absolutely vital difference. (In the special study on Authority in God's Kingdom, see the section on the Nature of Authority.)

2. The Apostle Paul was a master at leading others through relationships, and this truth is perhaps illustrated best in the very young church at Thessalonica. Notice from 1 Thessalonians just how he worked through relationships to keep them strong and growing even though he had been with them physically for only about three weeks.

   a. He freely expressed appreciation for their relationship and their work (1:2–9). As a leader, are you a charter member of the smile and compliment club?

   b. He explained his motives (2:1–6a). He neither demanded trust nor assumed it—he *built* it!

   c. He loved them with a mother's type of love (2:6b–9).

      (1) One, he was *gentle*. Others were not intimidated in his presence.

      (2) Two, he was *delighted* to share not only the message but his life. Now we are talking real family. Just how well do your people know you? The answer—only as well as you help them to know you!

      (3) Three, he worked *night and day* in order to benefit them most. Working hard for others is one thing; working hard *happily and gratefully* is yet another thing!

   d. He loved them with a father's type of love (2:10–12).

      (1) As the father is to lead the family, Paul set the righteous example that should characterize a father.

      (2) He encouraged, comforted, and urged them to live worthy lives. Fathers are the bottom-line sort of people who do not let *sentimentality* overrule *reality*!

   e. He recognized and identified with their problems (2:14; 3:2-5).

LOVE
One
ANOTHER

(1) It is true that a sentimental leader is not very helpful in the long run, but neither is an unsympathet-
ic one.

(2) Trying to motivate those who do not think you
really understand their struggles is a difficult task
indeed.

(3) Telling someone, "You shouldn't feel that way"
without really hearing them out is insensitive at
best and devastating at worst!

f. He demanded righteous living (4:1–8).

(1) As is often the case, he dealt with the area of sexuality and sexual temptations.

(2) Because of the nature of our sexual drive and of
the nature of our world, a wise leader deals with
this sensitive area directly and consistently.

g. He motivated them to love each other (4:9–10).

h. He kept them focused on heaven (4:13–18).

i. He warned them of Judgment (5:1–11).

j. He reminded them to always work on attitudes (5:12–
28).

(1) One attitude concerned their appreciation for
leaders. It is misplaced humility to shy away from
teaching on the subject. The very nature of leadership means that we are the very ones who must
teach such appreciation.

(2) The three succinct commands in vv 16–18, if followed seriously, would change any person's life
overnight!

III. The Sensitivity of Leadership

A. Sensitive in *manner.*

1. Although there are times to be very firm with the volume turned up, this approach will not be the norm (except in public preaching or teaching where the size of the crowd makes it appropriate and necessary.

2. When we are strong in manner, it—should be controlled and purposely used to help people come to convictions and repentance.

   a. The problem with many leaders (in fact, with most people in general) is that we have only *gear one* and *gear three*!

      (1) Gear one is the nice conversational tone in which we talk much of the time—not very direct or confrontational.

      (2) Gear three is very confrontational but is mostly misused—we stay in gear one as conflict avoiders until we cannot hold it in any longer, and then we blow up and blow people away.!

   b. In the Kingdom, we need to function most of the time in gear two—that mode of directness and honesty which addresses the issues straight on in a calm, reasonable manner.

3. An excellent passage that deals with manner in leadership is 2 Timothy 2:23-26. Study it out with the above thoughts in mind.

B. Sensitive in dealing with *opinion differences.*

1. In the Special Study on Authority, see the section entitled The Extent of Authority. It makes some important distinctions about the level and nature of leadership involved, and how all of that impacts *advice* and *command.*

2. Romans 14 is the classic text for such a consideration.

    a. There is room in the kingdom for differences (vv 1–8).

        (1) The challenge is in knowing which things belong to the realm of opinion and which belong to the realm of faith!

        (2) In areas of opinion, we need to live by our own consciences and avoid dogmatism.

    b. There is no room in the kingdom for judgmental attitudes (vv 9–12).

        (1) Narrow-mindedness and self-righteousness were condemned strongly by Jesus.

        (2) We must keep our hearts united in spite of differences and the tensions they can cause.

        (3) When the Bible specifically teaches something, it is binding and must be followed.

        (4) When the recognized leaders of a congregation set policies, it should also be viewed as binding and thus followed. (Hebrews 13:17 deals with such leadership.)

        (5) On the other hand, advice for individuals in areas of opinion is not in the same category. However, our attitudes must lead us *strongly* toward *agreement*, not toward differences—it is an issue of heart and unity. (In the Special Study on Authority, see the last section on The Response to Authority.)

    c. There is no room in the kingdom for examples that destroy (vv 13–23).

        (1) We should not exercise our liberty in a way that causes a weaker brother to stumble.

        (2) And we cannot violate our own consciences.

3. Consider the following questions in being prepared to lead and follow in a spiritual manner:

   a. In giving advice and direction, is your approach to teach the other person *how* to think, or to do their thinking *for* them?

   b. How can someone not follow advice without being independent and/or rebellious?

   c. What is your response when the advice you give is now followed?

   d. Are you comfortable giving someone you disciple or otherwise lead the *right of appeal* (to a higher leader)?

   e. What is the correct way to handle such an appeal as the one leading? As the one being led?

4. Your answers to these questions will tell you a *great deal* about your leadership, your followership and your heart! Don't take them lightly!

C. Sensitive in dealing with *confidentiality*.

1. Without question, this area is very important and yet somewhat complex.

   a. On one hand, confidentiality is a *must* in building trust and helping people.

   b. On the other hand, in order to help them in some situations, we may need to get advice and help from someone else who is more experienced or otherwise qualified than we are.

   c. Therein lies the dilemma, and it is onethat must be handled correctly and wisely.

2. A good place to begin is by applying the Golden Rule!

   a. When we have opened our hearts and lives to someone, we normally would not be comfortable knowing that they were sharing sensitive information with others,

LOVE
One
ANOTHER

unless we had approved such sharing in advance.

b. Normally newer disciples are more uptight along these lines than are more mature disciples who fully understand the need for a high degree of openness and are comfortable with it.

c. However, the issue is not what *you* might be comfortable with—the issue is how *they* might feel. The best thing to do is to be overly cautious and to ask them how they feel about others knowing the information you think needs to be shared.

(1) On the other hand, all disciples should grow in their understanding of the value of the kind of openness that gains the most help for them and encourages others to be more open as well.

(2) James 5:16 cannot be limited to only a very private setting. Once we know that Satan works best when we are *not* open (John 3:19–21), then we will want to get our lives out into the light and rejoice that we can no longer be *blackmailed* by anyone! That is real freedom!

3. Whatever else may be said, no leader or disciple can ever slip over the line of wisdom and become guilty of *gossip or slander.*

a. In Proverbs 11:13, a *gossip* is defined as one who betrays a confidence. The *intent* of the one talking is not at issue in the passage—only the *result* is!

b. In Ephesians 4:29, all unwholesome talk is forbidden, and is then contrasted with talk that is helpful for building others up and for benefiting those who listen.

c. In 1 Peter 2:1, *every kind* of slander is forbidden. If you are not sure if it's slander or not, it probably is!

4. Before sharing details about another person's life in a

potentially sensitive area without their knowledge, ask yourself the following questions:

    a. *Why* are you considering sharing these things?

    b. Will your sharing benefit the one you are sharing about?

    c. Will it benefit the one with whom you are sharing?

    d. Does the Golden Rule fit the situation?

5. When and how do you share about someone in order to obtain more help for them?

    a. When you really do need additional advice in order to provide the help that the person needs.

    b. In such cases (and they are reasonably common), clear it with the person before you proceed further.

    c. In the event that the person is uncomfortable with you sharing with anyone else, respect their feelings, but at the same time, continue helping them to see the value in obtaining the most help possible.

    d. When they are experiencing some difficulties with another person and find it hard to go to the person in order to work out the difficulty (as Matthew 5:23–24 and Matthew 18:15 demand), go with them and act as a facilitator.

    e. The only exception to these confidentiality guidelines would involve situations where the person's spiritual or physical life is in absolute danger, or they are implicated in an illegal matter of a serious nature.

6. What are the *exceptions* and *procedures* to follow when the issue is serious sin and not simply obtaining help for needed growth in a weak area of one's life?

    a. Legally, even a professional counselor is *not bound* to confidentiality when someone's life is at stake, and he is *required* to break confidentiality in a number of cases where illegal activities have occurred.

b. Spiritually, if someone in the church is engaged in a type of sin that will clearly cost them their soul, they must be helped to see the need for a broader involvement of people who can help them.

c. Biblically, when a person's sin is of a nature that church discipline is demanded by God, other leaders will have to be brought into the situation. Matthew 18:15–17 and other similar passages, really leave no choice except to bring others in.

7. An observation about the need of information by the ministry staff

a. The ministry staff does need to be informed about certain situations that affect the entire congregation or a significant portion of it. (In 1 Corinthians 1:11, Paul mentioned that some people from Chloe's household had informed him of serious problems in the Corinthian church—and he was thus able to act on the information in order to protect the church.)

b. Therefore, the members of the congregation have to exercise *trust* that these leaders will handle these situations, and the people involved in them, in a spiritual way. The staff has one goal—to help the disciples under their care to do and to be their very *best* for God!

c. And these leaders will have to be responsible with that trust, still observing the Golden Rule in the process.

8. One final observation is needed on the subject.

a. When sin has become such that church discipline has to be exercised, the person (and at least the general nature of their sin) will be made public within the group with whom they are most closely associated—

usually, their regional group.

b. In the event that someone has become a public enemy of the church, the church must be publicly *warned*
for their own spiritual protection. Along these lines,
consider the mention of a number of such enemies by
name in the New Testament (1 Timothy 1:20; 2 Timothy 1:15; 2:17; 4:10,14; 3 John 9–10).

IV. The Response to Leadership

A. Respond with *respect and appreciation.*

1. 1 Thessalonians 5:12–13 gives some good direction along
   these lines.

   a. Verse 12 tells us to respect them for their hard work,
   for their role, and for their being concerned enough to
   admonish you.

   b. Verse 13 tells us to hold them in the *highest* regard in
   love because of their work.

2. Hebrews 13:17 also has some very appropriate directions
   for us as followers.

   a. We are to obey them (literally, be *persuaded* by them).

      (1) The kingdom is a volunteer army, and no one can
      force you to obey. God tells us to make the *choice*
      to obey and submit.

      (2) Even God does not *force* anyone to obey him, be-
      cause his greatest delight is when we joyfully sub-
      mit out of our love for him. The same principle
      inheres when obeying human leaders.

   b. Since God charges them to keep watch over you and
   give an accounting for you, be cheerful and coopera-
   tive!

    (1) In this way, their work will not be a *burden*, but rather a real *joy*.

    (2) What kinds of things do you think *would* be a burden to your leaders?

    (3) What kinds of things do you think would bring them *joy* as leaders?

B. Respond by helping to *share the load*.

1. One way to help with the load is to not *add to it* by being a burden. Be a part of the solution rather than a part of the problem!

2. Another way to help with the load is to shoulder more of it—aspire to *leadership*.

    a. Many things can kill our desire to go into leadership at the highest level of which we are capable.

        (1) Some of the reluctance may be our own sin (laziness, fear, materialism, selfishness, etc.).

        (2) Perhaps you have known some leaders who seemed to be more burdened than joyful in their leadership.

        (3) Maybe your leaders have failed to impress you with the need for more and better leaders in the Kingdom. Be impressed—the need is *great* and it will *always* be great if the world is to be reached in our generation!

    b. Jesus was a leader. If we are to be like him, we must aspire to leadership at the highest level in which we can function effectively. You have but one life to live, and you have but one life to give—use it to make the most impact possible on ETERNITY! AND TO GOD BE THE GLORY!

LOVE
One
ANOTHER

CHAPTER FIVE

LOVE:
Disciplined by Limiting Relationships

INTRODUCTION

1. In this lesson, we are going to consider the topic of church discipline, or as it is often called, withdrawal of fellowship.

2. This topic is obviously not a pleasant one, but it is a necessary one and a biblical one.

3. In Protestant churches, the concept of church discipline has often been called the forgotten commandment.

4. In most churches, including ours, the concept could accurately be called the misunderstood commandment.

5. Therefore, our task will be to clear up both ignorance about the subject and misconceptions surrounding it.

I. What Is Church Discipline?

A. In a broad sense, it includes all efforts to train Christians in the way of the Lord (just as the discipline of children includes all training).

B. In the more specific sense that we are considering, it means the purposeful exclusion of a church member from the fellowship of other Christians because of unrepented sin after biblical procedures have been followed.

C. To those who have not studied what the Bible has to say on this subject, this definition may sound unloving, judgmental or harsh. However, the Bible rules out any of these responses as being valid.

1. In Proverbs 13:24, we are told that the one who withholds punishment from his child actually *hates* the child. The same would be true in the case of spiritual children.

2. Although a type of judging is forbidden by God (Matthew 7:1–2), the judging that would relate to church discipline is clearly *demanded* by God (1 Corinthians 5:12–13).

3. As to the charge of harshness, consider some of God's disciplinary actions in the Bible.

   a. In the Old Testament, we have the accounts of the Flood, Sodom and Gomorrah, Achan, Korah, Dathan and Abiram, and many others like them where God was very direct and very strong in his response to sin.

   b. In the New Testament, God's customary approach is to wait until the Judgment before dealing directly and forcefully with sin, but the case of Ananias and Sapphira in Acts 5 should convince that the nature of God and his hatred of sin has not changed in our day.

   c. After looking at such accounts, it becomes obvious that most of us do not see clearly both the kindness and the sternness of God (Romans 11:22).

D. Key biblical texts

1. Matthew 18:15–17

   a. If your brother sins against you, go to him privately for the purpose of bringing about reconciliation between the two of you. (The phrase *against you* is not necessarily in the original Greek manuscript.)

   b. If he does not repent, take others with you in attempting to resolve the situation.

   c. If this approach fails, share the situation with the church.

   d. Ultimately, lack of repentance demands that withdrawal of fellowship be practiced.

2. 1 Corinthians 5:1-13

   a. The sin here is sexual in nature, as a man was sleeping with his father's wife (evidently his stepmother).

   b. The church failed to deal responsibly with the sin— they were prideful about the matter (proud of their *understanding of grace*?).

   c. Paul's response was unmistakable: "But now I am writing you that you must not associate with anyone who calls himself a brother but is sexually immoral or greedy, an idolater or a slanderer, a drunkard or a swindler. With such a man do not even eat" (v 11).

3. 2 Thessalonians 3:6, 14

   a. In this context, Paul was addressing a situation where some people in the church were idle and not even looking for work.

   b. The first response to the problem was to refuse to feed such a person—*no work, no food* (v 10)!

   c. The second response was to take special note of this idle person who refused to obey Paul's instructions, and to stop associating with him *until* and *unless* he repented.

4. Other passages will be dealt with farther on in the lesson, but these provide us with clear directions about the need for, and nature of, this type of church discipline.

II. Which Sins Necessitate Withdrawal?

A. Some sins are mentioned specifically in this connection.

1. As we have already seen, both idleness and immorality are grounds for withdrawal (unless repentance occurs).

2. In 1 Corinthians 5:11, in addition to the sexual immorality, other sins are also listed, including *greediness, idolatry, slander, drunkenness,* and *swindling.* (In passing, it is interesting to ask how Christians would recognize the sin of *greed* in another's life? Materialistic attitudes would be a part of the answer, but the level of financial contribution would be involved as well.)

3. In Titus 3:10, a divisive person is to be warned once, then a second time, and if repentance is not produced, then the church is to have nothing to do with him.

4. In Romans 16:17, those who cause divisions by their false teachings are to be watched and avoided.

   a. In this passage, Paul does not state that the divisive false teachers are in the fellowship of the church, nor that they are to be excluded from such. Neither does he mention any action to be taken in reaching out to them or warning them.

   b. Therefore, he apparently left this issue somewhat undefined in order to allow the directions in the passage to be applied as needed—to *anyone* causing divisions and putting obstacles in the way of Christians.

LOVE
One
ANOTHER

_____
_____
_____
_____
_____
_____
_____
_____
_____
_____
_____
_____
_____
_____
_____
_____
_____
_____
_____
_____
_____
_____
_____
_____
_____
_____
_____
_____
_____
_____
_____
_____
_____

    c.   The passage will fit a *member* of the church who becomes destructive to the faith of others, a former member who is destructive, or even a total *outsider*.

    d.   The focus is not specifically on the *identity* of the sinful person, but rather on the *damage* he is causing—which cannot be neglected.

B. Some sins are not specifically identified with withdrawal, yet are included by necessity because of their impact on a person's relationship with God.

   1.   Withdrawal of fellowship is actually a recognition that a person has *already* lost fellowship with God due to unrepented sin.

   2.   Therefore, the church cannot be in fellowship with someone who is out of fellowship with God.

   3.   Many sins would qualify for this category, because most of the sin lists end with admonitions like this: "Those who live like this will not inherit the kingdom of God" (1 Corinthians 6:9–10; Galatians 5:19–21).

   4.   Obviously, not all sins are easily observed and some may never be seen by other disciples. But in this case, God will ultimately handle those situations, as 1 Timothy 5:24 states: "The sins of some men are obvious, reaching the place of judgment ahead of them; the sins of others trail behind them."

   5.   In the sin passages and the discipline passages, it is abundantly clear that known, unrepented sin cannot be tolerated by the church.

III. What Is the Procedure for Withdrawal?

A. Pray for the person (1 John 5:26).

B. Go to them and try to turn them back (Matthew 18:15–17; James 5:19–20).

1. Go in a spiritual manner (Galatians 1–2). Be gentle, careful about your own life (not self-righteous), and willing to help carry whatever burden the one in sin is carrying.

2. Take others (leaders) with you as the needs dictate.

C. Warn them (1 Thessalonians 5:14; Titus 3:10).

D. Finally, after they have been warned and refused to heed the warning, the church must now be warned and told to stay away from those in sin.

E. After they are formally withdrawn from, no social fellowship is permitted (Matthew 18:17; Romans 16:17; 1 Corinthians 5:11; 2 Thessalonians 3:14; Titus 3:10).

1. What is our attitude toward them now? Do not regard them as an enemy (2 Thessalonians 3:15).

2. What can we do to help them at this point? Continue to pray for them, and when you do see them, warn them as fallen brothers (2 Thessalonians 3:15).

IV. What Are the Purposes for Withdrawal?

A. To obey God—he commands it!

B. To keep the church pure—in two ways:

1. One, to protect the church from sinful influence (1 Corinthians 5:6)

    a. In this passage, sin is compared to yeast, which works through an entire batch of dough.

    b. Once unrepented sin enters the Body through one person, Satan gains easier access into other members of the Body. There is a spiritual principle involved that is subtle to the casual observer, but *devastating* in its results over a period of time.

  c. When sin is not purged, it leads to a *toleration* of sin, and that toleration then leads to an *acceptance* of sin, and finally, the acceptance leads to the *practice* of sin!

 2. Two, to keep the church from guilt as an accomplice (2 John 9–11).

C. To serve as a warning to the church (1 Timothy 5:19–20)

D. To show the world that disciples are totally committed to living for God and his mission on the earth

 1. In 1 Corinthians 5:1, Paul was highly upset about their lack of example before the world—they were doing things worse than the world does!

 2. In Acts 5:1-10, God practiced some *church discipline* very directly when he killed Ananias and Sapphira.

  a. Great fear seized the whole church *and all* who heard about these events (v 11).

  b. The church was highly regarded by the non-Christians (though they were afraid to join the church for a while!—v 13).

  c. Nevertheless, the church continued to grow *more and more* (v 14).

E. To restore the fallen Christian if at all possible

 1. Notice the hopeful wording in the following passages: Matthew 18:15; 1 Corinthians 5:5 (see 1 Timothy 1:20 for similar wording); 2 Thessalonians 3:14; James 5:19.

 2. However, this highly desirable result does not happen the majority of the time in real-life situations.

  a. When this serious act of discipline fails to move the person to repentance, the *Bible* has not failed; the church has not failed; God has not failed! Only the *person* has failed—they have failed to respond to the love of God expressed through the church (Revelation 3:19 —"Those whom I love I rebuke and discipline").

b. Withdrawal of fellowship is a last resort, much like an emergency operation. The odds are not good, but sometimes it saves a life and therefore must be tried.

c. However, even when repentance and restoration does not occur, all of the other purposes of such discipline are still accomplished! **The victory is still the Lord's, and to him goes the glory!**

LOVE
One
ANOTHER

_____
_____
_____
_____
_____
_____
_____
_____
_____
_____
_____
_____
_____
_____
_____
_____
_____
_____
_____
_____
_____
_____
_____
_____
_____
_____
_____
_____
_____
_____
_____

CHAPTER SIX

LOVE:
Deepened by Family Relationships

INTRODUCTION

1. The church is the family of God and it is all about how to be family and how to have great families.

2. In this lesson, we are going to start with the broadest focus, the church as family, and proceed to the narrower focuses of dating relationships, marriage relationships and finally, parent/children relationships.

3. Obviously, each of the topics could easily take up the entire chapter all by themselves (or the entire booklet, for that matter).

4. Therefore, we will concentrate on what makes each of these relationship categories so very special in the kingdom of God.

5. We will look at what they are (which is already superior to similar relationships in the world), but also at what they can become (which is very far superior to even what many of us are presently experiencing)!

6. The great promise of God is that life on every plane with him can exceed all that we ask or imagine. For

us, the kinds of relationships we will be discussing are closer to our hearts than almost anything else in life, and thus this promise of God is good news indeed!

I. The Big Picture—Here Are My Mother and My Brothers (the church as family)

A. Some of the most amazing words that Jesus spoke had to do with just how precious relationships in the church were to be.

1. In Mark 3, after Jesus' own family thought that he was *crazy* (vv 20–21), we find these words: "Then, he looked at those seated in a circle around him and said, 'Here are my mother and my brothers! Whoever does God's will is my brother and sister and mother'" (vv 34–35).

2. In Mark 10, when Peter was feeling insecure about really being able to be saved, Jesus assured him that when we sacrifice physical possessions and relationships for him and the Kingdom, then we will receive brothers, sisters, mothers, fathers and children in this *present* age (vv 29–30).

   a. Because of the age differences in the church, both physically and spiritually, we truly function as family members on every level for one another.

   b. Most of us were raised in families where our emotional needs were not met at the level intended by God, but *now* we can have what we missed out on earlier. *Praise God!*

   c. One of the most special blessings God has given me is the exalted privilege of being a *dad* to hundreds of younger disciples.

d. All of us have to gain a fuller understanding of just how blessed we are with these kinds of relationships, and then out of extreme gratitude, become more for each other than we have ever been!

B. In spite of the wonderful blessings offered to us in the family of God, some cautions are necessary to make sure we relate as he desires.

1. We can easily be focused on *taking* in relationships rather than *giving*, for several reasons.

   a. When our needs have not been met growing up, we can come into the church with some very deep-seated expectations that are not realistic, even in the family of God.

      (1) In such situations, our emotional *neediness* can repel the very ones to whom we are looking for filling up our void. (They back off from us emotionally because they can *sense* that they are not going to be able to live up to our expectations and that we are going to become critical of them when such failure occurs.)

      (2) These emotional voids can make us very possessive of relationships, which produces envy and jealousy in us and the repelling of others as mentioned above.

   b. The opposite scenario occurs when we were raised in an environment where we were the center of attention in our families, and we are accustomed to being *catered* to. (In a word, we are just *spoiled*.)

   c. Sometimes we simply see the goodness of Christian relationships, as Jesus intended (John 13:34–35), but allow these to be more important to us than our relationship with God himself. Such a focus makes us *selfish*, not *selfless*.

2. The answer comes in our seeking of God as our *greatest* focus in life.

    a. Jesus loved people, but he actually received much more heartache from them than anything else. If he had been focused on having his primary emotional and spiritual needs met by them, he would have been absolutely *miserable*!

    b. Instead, he loved God with all of his heart, soul, mind and strength, and was then *able* to love his neighbor as himself.

    c. The prayer life of Jesus was intense because of how much he was focused on pouring out his life to serve others, not because he feared death or was filled with personal requests for his own life. (Are your prayers *others*-focused or *self*-focused?)

C. Some questions will be helpful to you in evaluating how well you presently understand true spiritual relationships in the family of God.

1. Do you find yourself waiting for others to initiate with you rather that really reaching out to them?

2. Are you often critical of others because of their failure to meet your needs?

3. Are you possessive of your relationships? Does it bother you when your closest friends have other really close friends with whom they want to spend time? Do you feel jealousy or envy?

4. Do you have difficulty with relationship changes—with building new ones when ministry changes make it necessary? In these situations, is it hard for you to give away your heart quickly?

5. When you serve others in some way, are you offended or otherwise hurt when they do not *reciprocate*?

6. Have you ever contemplated moving because of disappointment with relationships? Have you ever thought of leaving the church because of such disappointment?

7. ARE YOU A HAPPY PERSON?

D. Relationships in the church are special, and can be phenomenal, but they will only thrive when we believe and act on the principle that Jesus stated: *"It is more blessed to give than to receive"* (Acts 20:35).

II. A Narrowing Focus—Male and Female He Created Them (dating relationships)

A. The study of dating relationships is interesting for many reasons, but one key reason is that dating is a modern phenomenon, unknown in the pages of the Bible. Therefore, our study will be based on biblical principles, but also on some very practical, time-tested, proven life principles. (Obviously, God intended for the discipling process to fill in the blanks on this one for sure!)

B. The beginning point in this study is to recognize and admit some basic truths about where we really are on this subject.

1. Most of what we know when we come into the kingdom is *wrong*!

2. Worldly relationships are usually selfish, too focused on heavy romance, and preoccupied with sex.

3. In this area, we should assume that our feelings, no matter how strong, will most often be *untrustworthy*.

4. Therefore, we need to *ask* for much advice—and then we need to *take* it!

5. The leaders who are giving this advice did not pull their ideas on what makes for healthy dating out of thin air— they can give you many examples of those who did it right,

and sadly, many examples of those who did it wrong and paid the consequences. Trust their intentions and their experiences!

C. Relationships between males and females in the family of God must have as their primary focus the quest for friendships.

1. These relationships must begin as *casual* relationships. The world is very inept at cultivating pure, fun, friendly relationships with the opposite sex. Take it S-L-O-W-L-Y! Learn to be casual friends.

2. These relationships should progress to spiritual working relationships. Share spiritual insights, dreams, and appropriate struggles with each other, and share your faith with non-Christians when you are out on dates.

3. If the relationship should progress to the romantic stage, let it do so naturally and slowly, while you keep the focus on friendship and spirituality. And do not confine yourself to one person too quickly. Dating is one of the best ways to learn how to develop great Christian male/female friendships—take advantage of the opportunities. Then when you marry, you will have learned how to build highly rewarding brother/sister relationships, and this ability will be a rich blessing to you for the rest of your life!

D. A final word on the advice issue

1. Emotions are a wonderful blessing when developed and directed spiritually, but a *curse* when they are not.

2. Most of the time, when we are really emotionally tied in to some decision that is very significant to our lives, our feelings will not be a safe guide.

3. In these situations, we need to back off and obtain a lot of advice from mature spiritual leaders whom we can trust to be (*painfully*) honest with us.

4. An old song has this line in it: "It can't be wrong when it feels so right." Satan *loves* that line, because he has used the concept to destroy countless lives. It not only can be wrong—it often is. Do not trust feelings, especially when the stakes are so high. Trust God to use others to give you good advice. He and we want the very best for you!

5. Sometimes, because of the caution involved in getting dating advice, some have felt that they were untrusted.

   a. In one sense that is true and in another sense, it is not true.

   b. The issue is not a lack of trust in anyone's *intentions* or *heart*—it is an issue of having the right kinds of experiences.

   c. For example, I do not trust my son, Bryan, to do brain surgery on me! I totally trust his heart, his love for me, and his good intentions. But I do not trust his training and experience!

   d. Similarly, I do not trust the inadequate, or just plain wrong, experiences of most people's dating life before they were in the kingdom. Let's learn and re-learn how to date under the watchful eye of the God who loves us and wants the very best for us!

III. Tie the Knot—They Will Become One Flesh (the marriage relationship)

A. Keep the *right priorities* in your marriage.

1. In this sense, the same thing that makes for good spiritual health in individuals also makes for good spiritual health in marriages.

   a. Life's worries, riches and pleasures choke out spiritual life (Luke 8:14), but a united focus on God enriches a marriage greatly.

b. **Illustration:** Imagine God at the top of a triangle, with husband and wife being at the two other angles below. As each of them moves closer to God, they automatically move closer to each other.

2. What does it mean to keep spiritual priorities in a marriage?

   a. The value system of *each* partner is spiritual and not materialistic.

   b. Prayers together are a consistent part of the relationship, preferably on a daily basis (see 1 Peter 3:7).

   c. You work together as a couple in discipling and counseling less mature couples.

   d. You work together in evangelistic activities—sharing, relationship building and studying.

   e. You have a weekly discipleship time of at least two hours, which is focused and planned. See the following format as an example of what a good discipling time would include:

      (1) **Commendations and compliments:** Share what you really have appreciated in each other—make it a great time of encouragement!

      (2) **Areas of need/problems:** Share things that have bothered you about your wife/husband. Men—only one or two things, not a long list! After that, it's the wife's turn.

      (3) Plan your **calendar/schedules** for the week. Talk about areas of shared responsibility (child care, use of the car, etc.).

      (4) Talk about your **feelings**—goals, desires, dreams, frustrations, fears—things that really bring out your hearts and inner convictions.

      (5) **Household management:** Talk about needs

around the house (the Honey-do list)!

(6) **Children:** Talk about how each of you feels about how they are doing. Make sure that you are unified about discipline and other parenting concerns.

(7) Plan for **Family devotionals** and **discipleship times** with each of the children during the week.

(8) **Finances:** Make sure that adequate communication on all financial issues takes place, and that each of you feels unified about the financial decisions that are reached.

(9) Close out with a **great prayer together**!

B. **Keep the *right love* in your marriage.**

1. Love is a much misunderstood word, not only in our society, but more so in the church than many of us would think.

2. There are three important Greek words for love, which must be understood by Christian marriage partners.

    a. *Phileo*—the friendship type of love, indicating the warm feelings brought about by being in the company of the other person.

    b. *Eros*—the word from which we get our word erotic, denoting the sexual attraction type of love.

    c. **NOTE:** The combination of the two above words are what the world calls *being in love*. When a couple feels these things, they will probably contemplate marriage, and when they lose them, they will probably think of divorce. For our purposes, this combination of love types can be called *romantic* love.

    d. The most important word is *agape*—that commitment type of love, unconditional in nature (like God), which focuses on the needs of the other person and not on our own needs.

3. God's design is for our *agape* love to bind us together even when the other two types of love begin to wane. This relationship glue enables a couple to rekindle their romantic love over and over through the years, with never a thought of divorce!

4. The most complete definition of this agape love is found in 1 Corinthians 13:4–8a. Read this passage, substituting your name in place of the word love each time it is used. How well are you really loving your mate?

C. Keep the *right roles* in your marriage

1. Read Ephesians 5:21–33 and 1 Peter 3:1–7 for the basis of marriage roles.

   a. From these two passages, it is apparent that women have the most difficulty respecting and submitting to their mates. (And no wonder, considering what our society is saying about such things! But of course *their* way is producing very fulfilled and happy women, along with highly successful marriages—*right?*)

   b. Men have the most difficulty getting past their selfish natures and really serving their wives physically, emotionally and spiritually.

2. These roles must be followed if marriages are to be great and if each partner is to be pleasing to God.

   a. Perhaps the most challenging lesson comes when the other partner does not follow these directions in the word of God. Even if your partner fails *miserably,* your responsibility before God has not lessened one iota. Agape love is an *in spite of* type of love, not a *because of* type of love!

   b. These teachings may sound totally nonsensical to those in the world, but they will work. In fact, *nothing else* will work. It is not that these principles have been tried and found wanting—they have been difficult and not often tried!

D. Keep the *right communication* in your marriage

1. Communicate at a *feeling* level.

    a. Talking about people and things is the least vulnerable level, followed by talking about ideas and values, but the level that builds marriage relationships is to talk about one's feelings.

    b. Men, we typically have the biggest problem talking on this level. Our wives *want* and *need* this level of communication, and we *need* it whether we start off *wanting* it or not!

2. Communicate with *kindness* and *sensitivity*.

    a. The principles found in Ephesians 4:29–31 will *eliminate* fights and quarrels, to the exact extent we put them into practice.

    b. The principles found in 2 Timothy 2:23–26 will *end* quarrels once they have started, to the same degree that we follow them.

IV. Fill the Earth—Be Fruitful and Increase (the parent/child relationship)

A. The importance of parental *relationship*

1. In two-parent homes, the relationship between parents is absolutely vital to the well-being of the children in those homes.

2. Even if parents have otherwise great relationships with the children on an individual basis, if the parents have a poor relationship with each other, the children will grow up very insecure.

3. The *unity* between parents on all issues is more important than the actual specifics involved in nearly every case. A lack of unity will damage your children more than you can imagine.

4. Great marriages will produce great families, and they will reproduce the same in their children's lives later, because the children will have seen the correct role models and will therefore be able to imitate them.

B. The importance of parental *leadership*

1. Parents are to set the *example* spiritually for their children, but then they have to instill their *hearts* in them. See Deuteronomy 6:4–7 for some very practical directions on how to accomplish these things.

2. This leadership responsibility falls on both parents in a practical sense, but God holds the father in the family most responsible (Ephesians 6:4; Colossians 3:21). The fathers who abdicate this responsibility and leave it up to their wives will rob their children and put themselves under the displeasure of Almighty God! And that, brothers, is a *serious* matter indeed!

C. The importance of parental *discipline*

1. Discipline of children covers the entire range of what it takes to train them in the Lord. It should never be viewed as simply *punitive*, or even *mostly* punitive.

2. This training must be customized to the needs of each individual child, corresponding to their personalities, sinful natures and talents. Proverbs 22:6 makes this point and concludes with a wonderful promise, making all of our efforts totally worthwhile.

3. Look up the following passages in the book of Proverbs for some practical help in disciplining of children: 14:26; 20:7,11; 22:6,15; 23:13; 29:15.

   a. Much more needs to be said about discipline, especially regarding when and how to apply corrective discipline (punishment).

   b. The whole issue of spanking is colored by the physical

abuse situations all around us in society, and therefore needs much more explanation.

c. This issue, and many others included in the parent/ child relationship, needs our focus in the atmosphere of discipling relationships. Good books are available and helpful, but discipling relationships are the foundation for our further learning about this vital area. Let's all get the help that we need!

LOVE
One
ANOTHER

CHAPTER SEVEN

LOVE:
Delighted by Body-Role Relationships

INTRODUCTION

1. This lesson was saved until last for a very distinct reason—it should be the most *exciting*!

2. To get us started, let's ask a couple of questions. How important is *your* role in the church? How important are *you* to God? (Are these two questions related—does the answer to the second depend on the answer to the first?)

3. How important is a one-week-old baby in the running of a household (helping with the chores, answering the phone, etc.) compared to the help that a twelve-year-old child might be able to give in a family? How important is the one-week-old baby to the *parents*? (Less important than the twelve-year-old?)

4. Do you get the point? We often base our worth spiritually on how noticeable a role we have in the kingdom, and yet God simply does not view us in that way. Our worth before God is not based on what we *do*, but on *whose we are*!

5. Understanding the place of roles in the church will make us feel far better about ourselves, each other, God, and the kingdom in general.

6. That statement is a big one containing some large promises, so let's jump into the study, raise our understanding in a number of areas, and see what blessings God has in store for us!

I. Understanding the Situational Challenges

A. The challenges of differences among the disciples

1. We are all different from one another in many ways.

    a. Some of these differences pose no problem for us at all—in fact we glory in them. Some of the differences in this category are racial differences, cultural differences, educational differences, age differences, socio-economic differences, and others. We rejoice to be in a church where prejudices have been dealt with to such a large degree, for it is a great testimony to a world where all of these differences bring disunity and mistrust!

    b. On the other hand, we sometimes have trouble with the differences between us in the *spiritual* realm.

2. When others have talents that we do not have, or when they have successes that we do not have, it is easy to feel bad toward ourselves, toward them, or both!

    a. Frankly, some of us get so caught up in performance that we *cannot* perform effectively—our frustrations rule out faith, which in turn rules out effectiveness. Unless we learn to accept who we are, relax and enjoy life, our future in the Kingdom is not a bright one. (But God wants it to be, and he is able to make it bright —we have to learn to cooperate with him.)

b. If all trees were the same, or all flowers, or all animals, or if anything else in nature were completely alike, God's creation would not be nearly as exciting and rewarding! And we would be *disappointed*!

c. Would our Creator have taken such pains to provide the remarkable variety in his *physical creation*, and then have planned for all of *us* to be *just alike*? Hardly! We have much to learn about rejoicing in our differences, do we not?

B. The challenge of *effectiveness* in the mission

1. Our basic mission in life as disciples is very clear—we are to make disciples, to seek and save the lost.

2. Therefore, we all have the charge of accomplishing this tremendously important task. But are we to accomplish it in exactly the same way? That is the big issue!

a. For the most part, we think that the approaches to being effective in evangelism must be the same for everyone. (Does not the discipling process involve learning from another person and imitating them?)

b. While learning from others and imitating them are valid parts of growth, they are not rigid and mechanical principles. We learn and we imitate, but we are still *ourselves*, and the learning must fit into who we really are as human beings.

c. The key is knowing what in us can and should be changed (as far as approach and method are concerned), and what in us must be a continuing part of who we *are* as people.

3. The way that we will be most effective is to have a disciple's heart, want to learn as much as possible from *whomever*, to try everything that we can to be effective, but then to

look for what seems to be the most natural, most effective way for us as individuals.

4. The problem is that when we try to be a square peg in a round hole, past the point of being able to *change* into a round peg, then we become bland, unmotivated and even more ineffective.

C. The challenge of having a *healthy view* of ourselves

1. How we view ourselves is more than having a worldly concern about our self-esteem.

   a. If we do not have God's view of ourselves, then we will be neither healthy nor happy.

   b. However, we often base our view of self on the view others have of us (or that we *think* they have) instead of the view God really has.

2. In the kingdom, some views have not been the best, although the *origin* of these views is quite understandable.

   a. For example, in a church planting, the need for ministry staff people is pressing. Thus much emphasis is understandably placed on going into the *full-time ministry*.

   b. The problem arises when a person who is not suited for the ministry (for any one of a number of valid reasons) begins to feel like a second-class citizen of the kingdom.

   c. Actually, even the term *full-time ministry* contributes to the problem, and leaves a misleading (nonbiblical) impression.

      (1) All disciples have a ministry (2 Corinthians 5:18), and all disciples are to be *full-time* (living) sacrifices (Romans 12:1).

      (2) Therefore, all disciples are in the full-time ministry in a real sense of the word!

(3) The accurate distinction to be made is that some are *church-supported* and others are *self-supported*—but we are *all* full-time ministry people in a definite sense.

(4) Is this distinction simply a trivial matter of terminology? Or, is it much more than that, affecting the way we see ourselves and therefore, affecting our effectiveness for the Lord? (For the answer to these questions, consider the struggles that the majority who get out of *church-supported* ministry go through—the way they now view themselves often takes a nosedive!)

d. Another related misconception arises when a congregation is in the role of sending out many foreign mission plantings. Those who are not chosen to be a part of a team (whether in or out of the church-supported ministry) also can struggle with feeling like second-class citizens.

(1) When a congregation has the role of sending out foreign plantings, the leaders must emphasize the need for *going foreign*.

(2) However, such an emphasis must be done in a way that those who do not go still feel like a vital part of the team and in no way *inferior*!

3. The answer to these difficulties is to cultivate a correct view of our value, based on sound biblical principles. If we base our significance on the type of role we have or on our performance level, we will slip into the same mold that the world uses.

D. The challenge of *appreciating* the strengths of others

1. This challenge can be fully met *only* when we meet the above challenges first.

a. When we feel good about our differences, then we also appreciate each other's strengths.

   (1) On a football team, a running back may struggle with another running back who is vying for his position, but he is totally fired up about great talent on the offensive line!

   (2) On God's team, no one is vying for our position, because God has as many positions as he has disciples—a tailor-made plan for every one of us!

b. When we love the mission of Christ and comprehend even a portion of the magnitude of the task before us, another's effectiveness causes us to rejoice and appreciate their God-given talents.

c. When we see ourselves as God does, we have peace rather than anxiety, and we are then freed up to appreciate the strengths of our brothers and sisters. (When a person receives a more than fair share of an inheritance, he feels great about someone else receiving their share.)

II. Understanding the Biblical Principles

A. Romans 12:1–8

1. The *background* and context of the book of Romans up to this point.

a. In chapters 1–8, Paul has developed in a systematic manner, the doctrine of justification by grace through faith. Then in chapters 9–11, he has applied that doctrine to their current situation of Judaism and how God viewed the Jews and how he had used them.

b. Now, in chapters 12–16, Paul applies the doctrine to the everyday lives of the disciples—*how should we then live?*

    c.   Granting the very careful way that he has developed the doctrine of how we are to be saved and to live, we would expect that Paul would end up at the point of elaborating on what Jesus said was the bottom line of everything—on the *greatest* commandments, to love God and to love our neighbors as ourselves (Matthew 22:36-40). And this he clearly does!

        (1) In vv 1-2, he describes what it means to love *God* with all of our hearts, souls, minds and strength.

        (2) In vv 9-21, he describes what it means to love our *neighbors* (in the church and out of the church).

        (3) In vv 3-8, he describes how to love (view) *ourselves*.

        (4) Only when we view ourselves in the right way are we able to view others in the right way. Hence, Paul discusses the greatest commandments in the most logical order—God, self and others.

        (5) Our focus needs to be on this part, which has to do with how we see our own lives and how we use them to love God and others.

2.   The *foundation* for our study of roles and gifts in the body —*love for God* (vv 1-2)

    a.   Shown by offering our bodies as living sacrifices—as the animal sacrifices had to die, so we are crucified with Christ and he now lives through us (Galatians 2:20; 2 Corinthians 5:15).

    b,   Shown by worshipping with reason, not ritual—*spiritual*, from *logikos*, means *belonging to reason*.

    c.   Shown by being transformed, not conformed—*transformed*, from *metamorphoo* (from which we get the English *metamorphosis*), means to *change to another form*. (See Matthew 17:2 and 2 Corinthians 3:18 for other uses of the word.)

d. Shown by being able to *discern his will* for us—in context, it means that we can understand our gifts and roles in the body.

3. *The application* to our roles in the body—in vv 3–8, Paul breaks this topic down into an issue of *humility*, an issue of *function*, and an issue of *gifts*.

    a. Humility (v 3) is a matter of seeing ourselves *soberly* (literally, *to be in one's right mind*)—who are we *really*? When we see God clearly (and the blessings of the salvation he has given us), then we can look at ourselves in the right way.

    b. Function (vv 4–5) means that we have different roles in the body because we belong to the others in the body, and they need all of the different body functions in order to be healthy (as in the case with our physical bodies).

    c. Gifts (vv 6–8) are described to some degree, not to fully list nor explain all of the gifts available in the body, but to demonstrate the view we are to have toward *ourselves*.

        (1) Nearly all of these gifts (with the exception of prophesying) are what we call natural, or nonmiraculous. They have been called *genetic* and *environmental* gifts. (In other words, we are born with some special talents or capabilities, and our environment has served to help develop them.)

        (2) All of the gifts are to be used for the purpose of serving others and not for serving ourselves in some way.

        (3) The gifts of the whole body *reveal* Christ. (Compare Colossians 2:9 with Ephesians 1:22–23—just as Christ revealed the fullness of God, the *church* reveals the fullness of Christ!) Therefore, leaving

out part of the gifts diminishes our representation and manifestation of Jesus Christ.

(4) Gifts and responsibilities are not the same thing. For example, not all have the *gift* of contributing, but all still have the *responsibility* of contributing. Those who *do* have the gift serve as examples for the rest of us to help us grow in this area and better carry out our *responsibility*!

(5) Let him **use** his gifts—a repeated idea here. We need to seek to use our own gifts, but we need to greatly encourage everyone else to use and develop their gifts (without pushing them past the point of their own faith—v 3).

B. 1 Corinthians 12:1-31

1   This particular section, in chapters 12–14, was written to address a type of division in the church at Corinth.

a.   The people in that church were very prideful and envious regarding their possession and use of gifts (mostly miraculous).

b.   Chapter 12 was designed to produce *humility*, chapter 13 was designed to produce *love*, and chapter 14 was designed to produce *common sense* and *order* in their services.

2.   Chapter 12 deals with gifts, but also with *roles*, through which the gifts were exercised. In a sense, the roles mentioned in the last verses of the chapter were also gifts from God, but generally speaking, roles are the channels through which gifts (*leadership* gifts in this case) are exercised.

3.   The main points in chapter 12 and how they promote *humility*:

a.   All gifts are *from God* (vv 1–6), therefore no man can boast.

(1) Verse 1 introduces the subject, and then vv 2–3 reminds the Corinthians that in their past, they had been led astray. Therefore, they needed to listen to Paul carefully to insure that ignorance did not cause them to be led astray again.

(2) Notice in vv 4–6 that the origin and nature of the gifts are described in terms of unity.

(3) The *origin* of the gifts traced back to the perfectly unified Godhead—the Spirit, the Lord and God.

(4) The *nature* of the gifts traced back to the *purpose* of the gifts—*service* and *working* (*gifts, service* and *working* are all interchangeable terms).

b. Every person's *specific* gift was determined by God (vv 7–11), so boasting is still ruled out.

(1) The gifts were given for the *common good* of the church.

(2) The gifts were given by the Spirit—it was and is a matter of grace.

(3) Whether the gifts were mostly miraculous (as in this passage), or mostly nonmiraculous (as in Romans 12), the lessons are exactly the same—*God* determined our gifts and not we ourselves.

c. We were saved in unity (vv 12–13), and our oneness makes us each part of a *team*, rather than a *prima donna!* We form *one* body, we were baptized into *one* body, and we were given the *one* Spirit to drink.

d. No member of the body is *inferior* (vv 14–20), which rules out pride.

(1) Feelings of worthlessness and inferiority are actually forms of pride.

(2) Whether our role *looks* important or not, God has determined it and says that it is important to the

good of the body.

(3) We are needed, but if we do not *feel* that, we tend to pull back and withdraw.

e. No member of the body is *superior* (vv 21–26), which also rules out pride (in an obvious way).

(1) If we feel superior, we will hurt others and squelch them due to our self-righteousness.

(2) We show *differing* honor or sympathy as the needs of one another dictate, but we have *equal concern*. (In other words, we treat a tragedy in the family of a nonleader with as much concern as a tragedy in the family of a leader!)

f. Finally, God appoints ordered leadership in the church (vv 27–31), and we simply need to accept it with humility (regardless of our own personal role). We need to quit thinking in a worldly manner and just *get happy!*

(1) The purpose here is not to give an exact ordering, for evangelists and elders are not even in the list, but rather to show the *need* for ordered leadership.

(2) The issue is that gifts and roles are determined by God for the good of the whole body, and that these roles have nothing to do with how important or valuable we are to God and to one another. To be even a *doorkeeper* in the house of God is an exalted *privilege* (Psalms 84:10)!

III. Understanding the Practical Applications

A. Application to leaders

1. Leaders need to *delegate*.

a. Gifts are to be *used*, Romans 12 emphatically says!

b. Leaders who do not delegate are either very prideful, very insecure or both.

c. No one leader has all of the gifts, nor does even a group of leaders—it takes every member of the body to form the fullness of Christ.

d. Therefore, leaders need to look for and develop gifts in others, and then use them to the fullest extent possible.

2. Leaders need to *seek input* regarding their lives and their leadership.

a. Since no one leader has all of the gifts, he not only needs to learn the fine art of delegation, but the *humble* art of seeking help!

b. Since he is surrounded by his own discipleship group for the most part, he needs to figure out a way to obtain input from the grassroots level on a regular basis.

c. He also needs to seek input (honest *critique*) from the other leaders around him, especially regarding his speaking and his leading of various types of meetings.

d. Failure to seek such input of ideas and critique will limit his effectiveness as a leader and therefore will limit the health and reproduction of the body as a whole.

3. Leaders need to *take some chances* in encouraging others to discover their gifts and put them into practice.

a. We are *not* discussing substituting some good deeds for evangelism in the case of *any* disciple!

b. We *are* making the case that a person working within the areas of his or her strengths will be both happier and more fruitful.

c. The same old approaches to ministry may seem safe and secure, but surely God would like to move our ministries faster and faster! Let them (do their thing) and let him (do his thing)!

B. Application to individual disciples

1. As individuals, we need to think about what we *do best* and *enjoy* the most in order to get a better idea of just what our gifts may be.

2. We also need to ask those who know us best what they think our greatest strengths are.

3. We should also take a look at our *inabilities* and come to terms with them.

    a. Some things in this area can change and should be worked on diligently in order to change.

    b. Other things in this area will likely never change significantly no matter what we do. If this seems the case to you and others who help you evaluate, then figure out a way to cover these inabilities and focus on maximizing your strengths! (Then you will be happier and more effective.)

4. Now it is time to take initiative, be creative and launch out to become who God made you in the first place!

C. Application to specific practical areas

1. We cannot provide a comprehensive list of all the possibilities within the practical areas, but we do want to provide enough to illustrate the point and to prompt much more thought in this direction.

2. Consider the area of **music**.

    a. An outstanding musician will be far more effective reaching out as a performer to other performers, or to those highly interested in his performance, than he will be at the local convenience store.

    b. This does not mean that he should not share at the

convenience store (those there may have no other contact with disciples), but it does mean that he will be far more confident and effective sharing in his own element.

c. In his element, he may be a star, but out of his element, he is likely less confident and less effective. Obviously, we all need to keep growing in our confidence in God to use us in any setting, but in our element, others will see us in a different way than they would in the streets, and they will respond differently as well.

3. Consider women who enjoy *aerobics or crafts* or any other area of interest to women in our society.

a. When they are around non-Christian women in their areas of mutual interest, they will be much more confident and effective in reaching out to them.

b. Again, no one is suggesting that cold contact evangelism should stop, but that we should all focus on areas of outreach that capitalize on who we are as people. Personally, when I am happy with my lot in life, doing what I do best, then my sharing is more natural and more sincere than when I am out of my element.

4. Consider the area of **public service**.

a. Matthew 25:31–46 makes it obvious that Jesus is very concerned with how we treat people who are physically needy, sick or in prison.

b. At the present time, many of our churches are involved in jail ministry and food pantries. They are visiting prisoners and studying with them, and they are feeding hundreds of people in their communities who need and appreciate the help.

c. Besides making a very good impression on those being helped, the communities are taking notice and desiring to help out in ways as well.

d. Question: Will the people in those communities be *more* open or *less* open to sharing from those who are serving like Jesus did (and like he told us to do)?

e. Question: Will those doing the serving be *more* likely or *less* likely to share about Jesus and their church?

f. Surely the answers to these questions are obvious. The serving Christians will be more excited to share their faith, the ones being served or watching the serving will be more open, and God will bless the efforts to imitate Jesus and his type of ministry with fruit!

5. Before the advent of mass evangelistic methods (blitzing, the *one-a-day challenge*, street preaching, campaigns, etc.), churches among our Movement still grew at good rates. *How?* About like we have discussed in the above material.

a. I do *not* doubt that God led us to methods of evangelism that enable us to reach out to large numbers of people that we may not reach in any other way.

b. On the other hand, I doubt *seriously* that he intended these to become a substitute for more natural, lifestyle, relationship evangelism.

c. Some of us are basically *isolationists* who dash out of our little comfort zones to invite one or two people to Bible Talk or church, and then dash back in to our protected environments feeling at least a little better about ourselves as disciples.

d. It is time to repent of our cowardice, take up our places in society as the *light* and the *salt* and the *leaven*, and start making disciples the way Jesus did—with all evangelistic approaches. But like him, we must seek the ones that work the best in our society.

CONCLUSION

God made us as very unique individuals, and he intends to use our uniqueness for the purpose of glorifying his name in a way that no one else can. We need to appreciate how he has made us and who he has made us, and then cooperate with him and the ones he has placed in our lives in order to become all that we are meant to be. Let's love God, one another, and our own role in the kingdom—whatever it may be at a given point in time. **Let's be delighted by body-role relationships!**

LOVE
One
ANOTHER

_____
_____
_____
_____
_____
_____
_____
_____
_____
_____
_____
_____
_____
_____
_____
_____
_____
_____
_____
_____
_____
_____
_____
_____
_____
_____
_____
_____
_____
_____
_____
_____
_____
_____

LOVE
One
ANOTHER

_____
_____
_____
_____
_____
_____
_____
_____
_____
_____
_____
_____
_____
_____
_____
_____
_____
_____
_____
_____
_____
_____
_____
_____
_____
_____
_____

SPECIAL STUDY:
Authority in God's Kingdom

I. The Need for Authority

A. In the organizations of men

1. In America (along with most of the rest of the world), society is bordering on chaos because of a breakdown of authority.

2. The deterioration of homes and schools is nothing short of amazing.

3. However, *no* organization can survive and flourish without authority.

B. In the organization of God

1. Without authority, God's nation suffered greatly—Judges 21:25.

2. Moses could not lead the nation without the support of many other leaders with authority (Exodus 18:13-26).

3. God placed leadership in the church in order to lead his people to maturity and productivity (Ephesians 4:11-16).

II. The Nature of Authority

A. Basic types of authority

1. *Relational*—a friend has some influence, a type of

authority, on our decisions.

2. *Knowledge*—we allow people with training and experience, like doctors, to exercise some type of authority in our lives (an authority of expertise).

3. *Positional*—the officer in the military or the boss of a company exercises authority simply on the basis of his position.

B. How these types relate to the question of authority in the church

1. Without doubt, authority in the Kingdom is to be *relational* in nature. Even though everyone in a congregation cannot know all leaders on an intimate basis, we must *see* each other as family and strive hard to *feel* family.

2. As far as the authority of *expertise* goes, more experienced leaders will exert more influence than will less experienced ones. However, in any family, the older brothers and sisters teach the younger ones many valuable things. Families were never designed for the parents to have to do all of the teaching. Surely this is also true in the family of God. Discipleship, as described in Matthew 28:19-20, is based on these principles.

3. What about *positional* authority in the church?

   a. Because of seeing a wrong exercise of authority, many religious people have concluded that every vestige of positional authority is to be avoided.

   b. While it is true that such authority does not exist in *isolation*, without being combined with the other types, positional authority *definitely* has a place in the kingdom.

   c. The purpose of this study is to clarify these issues both from biblical and practical viewpoints.

III. The Categories of Authority

A. Government—Romans 13:1–7; 1 Peter 2:13–17

B. Masters (Employers)—Colossians 3:22–24; 1 Peter 2:18–20

C. Husbands—Ephesians 5:22–25; 1 Peter 3:1–6

D. Parents—Ephesians 6:1–3

E. Church leaders—1 Thessalonians 5:12–13 (and the other passages to follow)

IV. The Key Texts of Authority

A. Matthew 20:25–28

1. The word for authority here is from the Greek *exousia*. Is Jesus ruling out all authority in the church?

   a. In v 28 here, Jesus is using himself as an example of the right kind of leader, a *servant* leader. Yet, he has all authority (exousia) in heaven and on earth (Matthew 28:18).

   b. In 2 Corinthians 10:8; 13:10, Paul claims to have the authority (*exousia*) of an apostle.

2. Obviously Jesus is not ruling out all authority in the church, but he is ruling out p*ositional only* authority (see 1 Peter 5:1–4).

B. Hebrews 13:17

1. The word *authority* in our translation is not in the Greek, so the literal translation would be "submit to them" (as leaders).

2. The word *obey* is from *peitho*, and the literal meaning is *"be persuaded."*

   a. Of course it is true that good leaders need to persuade

their people from the Scriptures and with reason, but this passage is not directed at leaders.

b. Followers are commanded to be persuaded. Just as no leader can make you submit if you do not have a submissive heart, no leader can persuade anyone who refuses to be persuaded. It is an issue of heart!

c. The same word is found in James 3:3, which reads: "When we put bits into the mouths of horses to make them obey us, we can turn the whole animal." (Not that people are horses or leaders should use bits, but the word is not a weak one in its biblical usage!)

3. Who are the leaders in this verse?

a. They are recognized congregational leaders with a designated work in the church, for which they will give an account. Therefore, make their work a *joy!*

b. To apply this passage to a six-month-old Christian discipling a two-month-old Christian could be hazardous to the spiritual health of both!

C. 1 Corinthians 16:15–16

1. The word submit in v 16 is from *hupotasso* in the Greek. It is also a strong word, as its usage in James 4:7 would indicate: "*Submit yourselves*, then, to God. Resist the devil, and he will flee from you."

2. This passage is an excellent one to show the natural ordering of a developing leadership.

a. The earlier converts became the early leaders, as would be expected, and should be submitted to as a result.

b. Also, all the others who joined in the work (as leaders) should be submitted to as well.

3. Some people have tried to escape the clear teaching of this passage by appealing to v 12 in the same chapter regarding

the unwillingness of Apollos to follow the urging of Paul.

   a. However, any appeal that sets one Scripture in contradiction to another is a very suspect appeal to begin with!

   b. The issue in this verse was not *whether* Apollos was going to do what Paul asked, but only when he was going to do it.

   c. We must also keep in mind that we are talking about two very influential leaders with different responsibilities, which had to be taken into consideration. Timing in ministry responsibilities is always a big issue.

   d. Comparing this situation with submission to leaders in a congregation is comparing *apples* and *oranges*.

   e. On the other hand, the passage does show the rightness of discussing differing opinions with the right spirit and even working out compromises (timing, in this case).

D. Evangelistic authority as seen in the letters written to evangelists

1. 1 Timothy 1:3–4; 4:1–12; 5:19-20; 6:17–18

2. 2 Timothy 2:14; 4:1–5

3. Titus 1:5, 7–14; 2:15; 3:10 (In Titus 2:15, *authority* is from *epitage*. The same word is translated in Titus 1:3 as *command*, command of God in this case.)

V. The Extent of Authority

A. Common sense and practical judgment are definitely required in many situations that are not "book, chapter and verse" issues.

B. Several issues are involved in determining the extent of authority in such situations.

1. The higher the level of *leadership*, the higher the level of *responsibility*. And, the higher the level of responsibility, the higher the level of *authority* must be. You cannot be held responsible for something without the authority to get it done!

2. Christian *maturity* is another key consideration. A very mature Christian, even at lower levels of leadership, would exert more influence generally than would a young Christian.

3. The *impact* of decisions on oneself and on others is another consideration.

   a. If the impact is *only* on the person making the decision, that is much different than making a decision that affects *many* people.

   b. Therefore, in one case, the input is more along the lines of *advice,* while in the other case, the input would be more along the lines of a *command.*

C. Authority in the church is obviously broader than simply enforcing specific biblical commands. Even in areas of judgment, leaders, decisions should be followed unless one of two conditions exists:

1. One, you are asked to violate Scripture (Acts 5:29).

2. Two, you are asked to violate your conscience (Romans 14:23). However, this condition must be real, and not simply an excuse to do your own thing!

VI. The Response to Authority

A. Submission is not:

1. Obeying only when you are in *agreement* with the direction given.

2. Obeying only *outwardly*, without the heart involved and the attitudes positive.

3. Obeying only when you think the leader has led in just the *right manner*.

4. Obeying without speaking your mind and sharing your viewpoint. *Stuffing* your feelings is not proper submission.

5. Obeying only a part of the directions given—*filtering* is deceptive and dishonest. If you are having difficulty agreeing with the directions, keep talking until you and the leader are in harmony.

6. In the area of seeking individual advice, it is not right to continue seeking advice until you find someone who will say what you want to hear. In such cases, you are likely sharing only the facts in the situation that will help you get your way. You should always be in harmony with everyone who gives you advice, even if you do decide to go in a different direction. Keep talking until everybody involved feels good about the situation. *Practice the Golden Rule!*

B. Submission is:

1. A willingness to be persuaded and to be unified with those leading.

2. A recognition that submission is a great producer of humility, and that God always blesses humility.

3. A deep conviction that God leads through the leaders whom he has raised up, and that to follow these leaders, human though they are, is to follow God.

LOVE
One
ANOTHER

LOVE ONE ANOTHER —QUIET-TIME SCHEDULE

SUGGESTED STUDY APPROACHES:

1. Since the Bible is designed to produce faith and then increase it, let's approach the lessons with that in mind.

2. According to Hebrews 11:6, faith is composed of three elements—belief, trust and obedience. We believe the facts of the Bible, we trust the promises, and we obey the commands. Keep these elements in mind as you do your daily Q.T.'s.

3. As you study, ask yourself the following questions (and write down the answers):

    (1) What new facts did I learn and which known ones were most helpful or convicting in the day's lesson?

    (2) What new promises did I learn about, or which known ones made a real impression on my heart?

    (3) Which commands made the most impact on me, and what will I do to obey in the way that God desires?

    (4) Overall, which lessons do I most need in my life at the present time? (Select only two or three and make a plan about how you are going to act on them today.)

    (5) Who can I share these applications and convictions with today, and when can I do it? (Please make sure that you follow through on this point— lessons shared are lessons kept!)

DAILY READING / STUDY SCHEDULE

Day 1:   Foreword, Introduction, Chapter One Introduction, and I. (Misused Sexuality).

Day 2:   Chapter One, II. (Materialism).

Day 3:   Chapter One, III. (Selfishness).

Day 4:   Chapter One, IV. (Pride).

Day 5:   Chapter Two, Introduction and Passages in Chronological Order (read).

Day 6:   Chapter Two, I. (Peace), and Observations About Peace

Day 7:   Chapter Two, II. (Love), and Observations About Love

Day 8:   Chapter Two, III. (Encouragement), and Observations About Encouragement

Day 9:   Chapter Three, Introduction, and I. (Biblical Basis)—A. and B. only.

Day 10:   Chapter Three, I. (Biblical Basis)—C. (Group Discipling) only

Day 11:   Chapter Three, II. (Powerful Purpose)

Day 12:   Chapter Three, III. (Healthy Heart)

Day 13:   Chapter Three, IV. (Priceless Practicals)

Day 14:   Chapter Three, (Confidentiality Section)

Day 15:   Chapter Four, Introduction, and I. (Design for Leadership)

Day 16: Chapter Four, II. (Motivation by Leadership)

Day 17: Chapter Four,, III. (Sensitivity of Leadership)

Day 18: Chapter Four,, IV. (Response to Leadership)

Day 19: Chapter Five, Introduction, and I. (Church Discipline?)

Day 20: Chapter Five, II. (Which Sins?)

Day 21: Chapter Five, III. (Procedure), and IV. (Purposes)

Day 22: Chapter Six, Introduction, and I. (Big Picture)

Day 23: Chapter Six, II. (Dating)

Day 24: Chapter Six, III. (Marriage)

Day 25: Chapter Six, IV. (Parenting)

Day 26: Chapter Seven, Introduction, and I. (Situational Challenges)

Day 27: Chapter Seven, II. (Biblical Principles)

Day 28: Chapter Seven, III. (Practical Applications)

Day 29: Appendix, Special Study on Authority in God's Kingdom

Day 30: Review all the *One Another* passages.

www.ipibooks.com